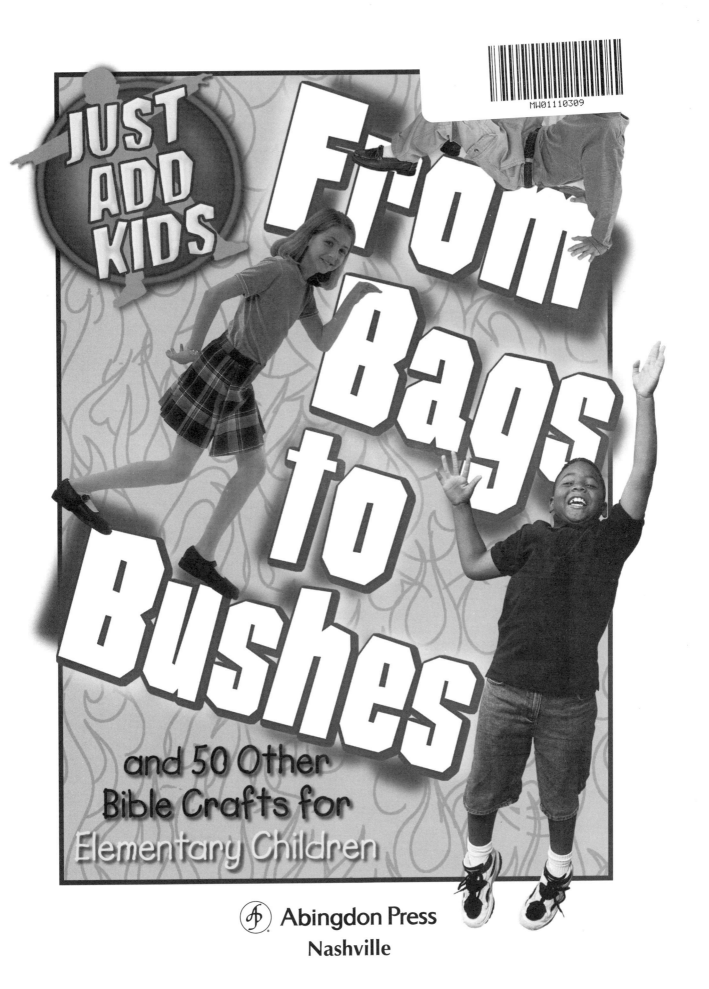

JUST ADD KIDS

From Bags to Bushes

and 50 Other Bible Crafts for Elementary Children

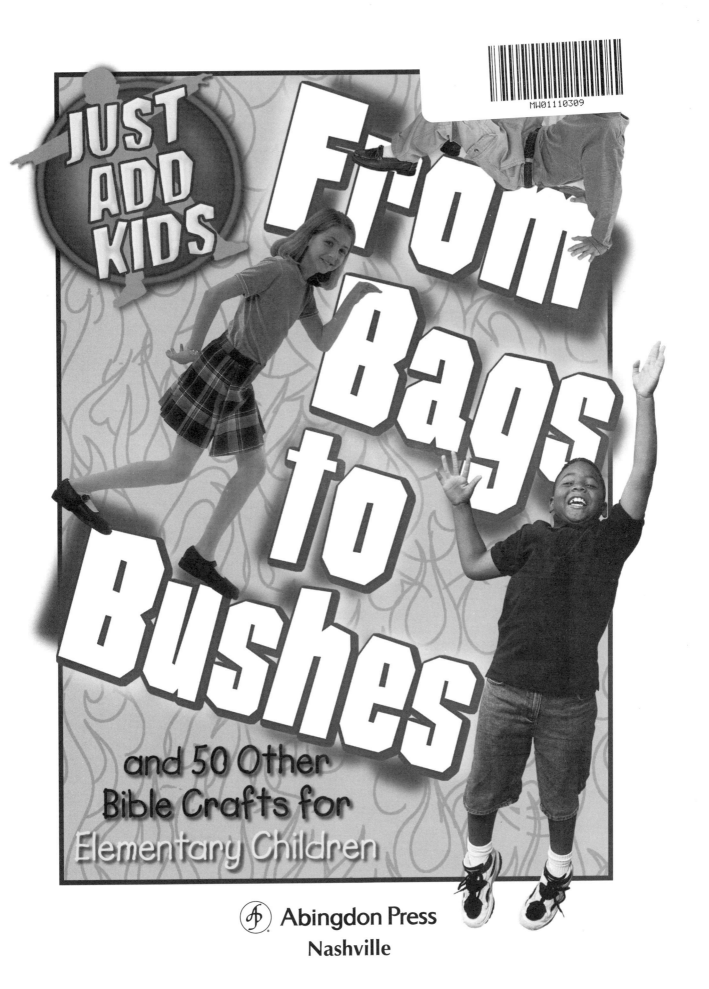

Abingdon Press

Nashville

Just Add Kids: From Bags to Bushes and 50 other Bible Crafts for Elementary Children

ISBN 0-687-04900-8

Unless otherwise noted, Scripture quotations are from the New Revised Standard Version of the Bible.
Copyright © 1989 by the Division of Christian Education
of the National Council of the Churches of Christ in the United States of America.
Used by permission. All rights reserved.

Scripture quotations identified as *Good News Bible*
are from the *Good News Bible: The Bible in Today's English Version.*
Old Testament: Copyright © American Bible Society 1976, 1992;
New Testament: Copyright © American Bible Society 1966, 1971, 1976, 1992.
Used by permission.

The purchaser of this book is entitled to reproduce ANY PATTERN,
provided the copyright notice is included.

Lead Editor: Daphna Flegal
Editor: Betsi H. Smith
Contributing Writers: LeeDell Stickler, Judy Newman-St. John, Marcia Stoner
Designed by: Paige Easter
Illustrated by: Megan Jeffery (page 32: Barbara Upchurch)
Cover Photographs: Ron Benedict

00 01 02 03 04 05 06 07 08 09—10 9 8 7 6 5 4 3 2 1

MANUFACTURED IN THE UNITED STATES OF AMERICA

ELEmentary Crafts
Table of Contents

3

4

Introduction
Welcome to Just Add Kids

Who hasn't seen the child leaving class, proudly carrying his or her newly made creation? "Look what I made!" the child will say over and over until someone does stop and look and praise the child for such a fine creation. Sometimes it seems that craft time is the only specific activity a child can remember, and there's a reason for that: Hands-on activity encourages learning.

From Bags to Bushes and 50 Other Bible Crafts for Elementary Children is loaded with crafts that your children will be proud to carry home. Many use reproducible pages, which are included here. And since each craft in *From Bags to Bushes* relates to a specific event in the Bible, your children are learning while they're creating.

Each child in your class is unique, with his or her own family background and experiences. But elementary children do have some common traits. Understanding those traits will help you in your classroom:

- They are restless and energetic, and would rather participate than watch or listen. Each one of them is growing at a different rate.
- They are concrete thinkers, but they are just beginning to develop an ability to reason and discuss. They are curious and have great imaginations.
- They are becoming less dependent on parents. They enjoy playing with other children, but will often imitate adults in their actions.

For guidelines on how to make the most out of your crafts time, see the article on the next page. For other resources that will help you make your class time the best that it can be, don't miss the other books in the *Just Add Kids* collection:

- *The Jailhouse Rocked and 50 Other Bible Stories for Elementary Children.*
- *Downright Upright and 50 Other Bible Games for Elementary Children.*
- *Don't Get Wet Feet and 50 Other Bible Stories for Preschoolers.*
- *Footprints on the Wall and 50 Other Bible Crafts for Preschoolers.*
- *Ring 'Round Jericho and 50 Other Bible Games for Preschoolers.*

Using Crafts to Teach God's Word

Children learn through creating. Whether it's painting, cutting, coloring, gluing, or squishing clay through their fingers, children are perhaps most like God the Creator when they are creating.

Follow these simple guidelines to make craft time a success in your classroom:

- **Create a craft center.** If possible, set up your craft center in an uncarpeted area. While tables may be obstacles in other areas of your classroom, they work well here. Keep basic supplies on hand: glue, tape, construction paper, scissors (safety scissors, if you have young children), crayons, markers, and so forth.

- **Plan ahead.** Gather all the materials the children will need to complete their craft. Some crafts will require photocopying, cutting, and even some assembly. You will want to complete these steps before class begins. Make the craft ahead of time so that you understand the process and can help your children, if they need it.

- **Make it messy.** Some of the best crafts are the messiest ones. You may not want to have a messy craft every time you meet; but add them occasionally, and just watch the children enjoy themselves. It's wise to keep paint smocks on hand. (These can be as simple as adult-size shirts that the children wear over their clothes.) Also have hand-washing supplies available. Keep cloths nearby during craft time to mop up any spills.

- **Make cleanup time a part of craft time.** Children love to help, so use that to your advantage when it's time for cleanup. Give the children specific instructions: "Cathy, please put the crayons back in the box. Bryce, please put the scraps of paper in the trash can. Jana, please put all the chairs back around the table." Be sure to thank the children for their help.

- **Give lots of praise.** Talk with the children as they work. Look for and compliment anyone who is sharing the craft supplies. Find words of praise for each child as he or she creates. Remember, especially with young children, the process of creating is much more important than the finished product.

Sun, Moon, Stars

Craft 1

Supplies: cardboard boxes, tape or glue; items such as packing peanuts, cardboard tubes, aluminum foil, masking tape, drinking straws, wrapping paper, small boxes, white glue, plastic wrap, stones, sticks, ribbon or yarn, cardboard sheets, and bottle lids

Box of Junk

Before the children arrive, collect a variety of junk items to place in medium-sized cardboard boxes. Put one box on each table. Make sure there are different items in each box so that the children cannot copy one another's creations. Some examples of items are packing peanuts, cardboard tubes, aluminum foil, masking tape, drinking straws, wrapping paper, small boxes, white glue, plastic wrap, stones, sticks, ribbon or yarn, cardboard sheets, bottle lids, and so forth.

Welcome the children as they arrive. Assign each child to a table. Each table should have no more than four children.

Say: God took a little bit of this and a little bit of that and created a world. I want each team to create something using all of the items that are included in your box. Don't leave anything out. When everyone is finished, we will share our creations.

When the children finish their creations, invite the group to come back together and let the groups share.

Ask: Was it fun to create something out of nothing? Was it hard? How did you decide what to use where? Do you ever wonder what God thought about as God made our wonderful world?

© 1999 Abingdon Press.

Bible
Genesis
1:14-18

Craft 2

Supplies: balloons, newspaper (cut into one-inch strips), wallpaper paste, acrylic paint, large mixing bowl, cover-ups, paintbrushes, safety pins, fishing line, clean-up supplies, globe, clear acrylic spray

My Own Personal Globe

Give the children a sense of the interdependence of our world as they create their own papier-mache globes. Have a globe on hand for the children to look at.

Have each child blow up a balloon and tie the end tightly. Place wallpaper paste in a bowl. Have the children wear cover-ups.

Show the children how to cover the balloon surface with three of four layers of paper strips dipped into the wallpaper paste. Leave the tied end sticking out of the covering.

Insert safety pins into the end of the balloons, being careful not to pop the balloons. Hang them on a clothesline to dry for several days.

When the balloons are totally dry, have the children pop them and pull them out through the small opening where the end of the balloons sticks out.

Let the children paint their balloons to represent the earth: green for the land; blue for the water. When they are dry, spray them with an acrylic spray and hang with fishing line.

God Created Animals

craft 1

Supplies: animal fronts and backs (see page 12), glue, drawing paper, crayons or markers

Fronts and Backs

Make a copy of the animal fronts and backs (see page 12) for each child in the group. Cut the sections apart.

Say: Today's Bible lesson is on the creation of all the animals. God created some pretty spectacular animals. God created large animals and small animals, animals with bright colors and animals with dull colors, animals that live in the air, in the sea, and on the earth.

Ask: If you had been in charge of creating animals, what would yours have looked like?

Give each child a set of fronts and backs. Let the children take apart and glue each animal front or back onto a piece of drawing paper. Then let each child "finish" the animal with crayons or markers. The children may give their animals names. Share the creations with the group.

Bible
Genesis
1:20-25

craft 2

Supplies: large, flat pieces of cardboard; pine lathe; white latex paint, paintbrushes; newspaper; variety of colors of tempera paint; scissors; camera and film; masking tape; markers

Giant Photo Op

Have the children recreate a scene from one of the Bible stories as a unique poster with real faces.

Check out discount and warehouse stores for large, flat pieces of cardboard. Staple strips of pine lathe (found at lumberyards or home center stores) to the cardboard for stability. Tape the joints on the back side only.

Let the children prime the cardboard with white paint. Use old latex house paint.

Sketch a scene from one of the stories. Draw in the faces as large as your own face. Have an adult cut the holes for the heads. Let the children paint in the scene. Display in the church narthex with the characters in place.

Let each group of three of four children choose a different story or scene.

Take pictures.

© 1998 Abingdon Press.

11

Permission granted to photocopy for local church use. © 1999 Abingdon Press.

In God's Image

Craft 1

Supplies: facial features (see page 15), six-inch paper plates, crayons or felt-tip markers, tape, white glue, construction paper, yarn

Funny Faces

Before class photocopy and cut apart the facial features (see page 15) for each child in the group. Set out the supplies.

Say: Today we are going to talk about the last act of creation—God's creation of human beings. When we look around us, we can see that there are many different kinds of human beings, all of whom look different from one another. Today I want you to create a funny face on the paper plate, using some of the features here, as well as adding a few creative touches of your own.

Let the children work to create a funny face. When everyone is finished, let the children share their faces with the group or mount them on a bulletin board.

Say: Just as each of you created an individual face, God created us as individuals as well.

© 1999 Abingdon Press.

Bible
Genesis
1:26-27

craft 2

Supplies: construction paper, writing paper, instant-developing camera and film, white glue, yardstick, bathroom scale, pencils, stapler and staples, crayons or felt-tip pens

A Book About Me

Have the children create a book about himself or herself. Each child can write or draw things that are important to him or her. Take each child's picture. Measure and weigh each child and let him or her list that information in his or her book. Encourage the children to draw a picture of where they were born and of their family members.

Make a cover from construction paper and glue the picture on the front of the book. Tell the children to save their books in a special place. They can take them out occasionally and compare the picture to how they have grown since the pictures were taken.

craft 3

Supplies: large sheets of black construction paper, strong light source, large sheets of white paper, pencil, white chalk or crayons, scissors, glue, tape or tacks

Silhouette Gallery

Hang a large sheet of paper on the wall or bulletin board. You will replace this with a new sheet after each child's silhouette is traced. Set up a silhouette booth. Place each child sitting sideways. Position the child between the large sheet of white paper and the light source. The child's shadow should be distinct on the paper.

Draw around the shadow. Let each child cut out his or her silhouette and then trace it with white crayon or white chalk onto black construction paper. Cut out the silhouettes and mount them on colored paper.

When every child's silhouette is on the wall, let the children decide who each one represents. It is even more fun to invite the parents and let them try to identify the children. Talk about what it means to be created in the image of God.

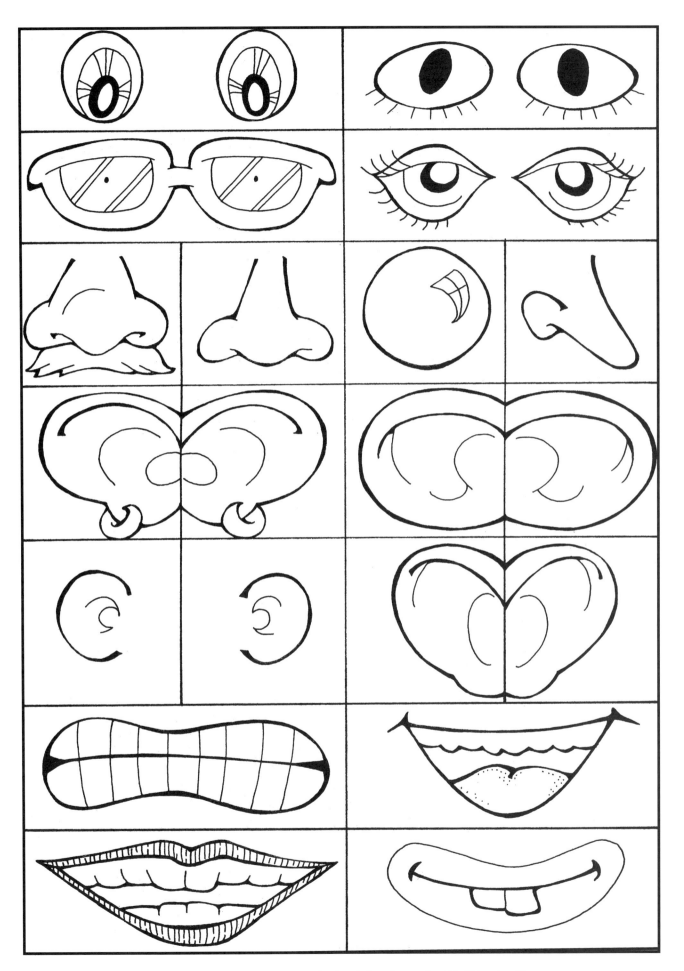

15

Garden of Eden

craft

Supplies: diorama figures (see pages 17 and 18), sturdy white or green plastic dinner plates, crayons, scissors, tape or glue

Garden in the Round

Make a copy of the diorama figures (see pages 17 and 18) for each child in the class.

Say: When God created the world, God also created the first man and the first woman. God placed them in a special garden called Eden. In this special garden was everything the man and woman could possibly need in order to live. God also placed the animals in the garden and told Adam to care for them.

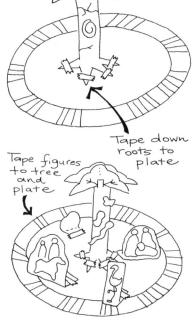

Tape down roots to plate

Tape figures to tree and plate

© 1999 Abingdon Press.

Have the children create a garden in the round using the figures on pages 17 and 18. Begin with a large sturdy white or green plastic dinner plate. Have the children color and cut out the figures.

Assemble the Tree of Life as shown in the illustration here. Add the serpent to the tree. Add the figures of the animals and Adam and Eve around the edges of the plate. Before adding the animals, the children with white plates may want to color their base plates green.

Say: God created the first human beings. God loved them and cared for them and provided all that they needed.

© 1999 Abingdon Press.

Bible
Genesis
2:8–10

Glue tab

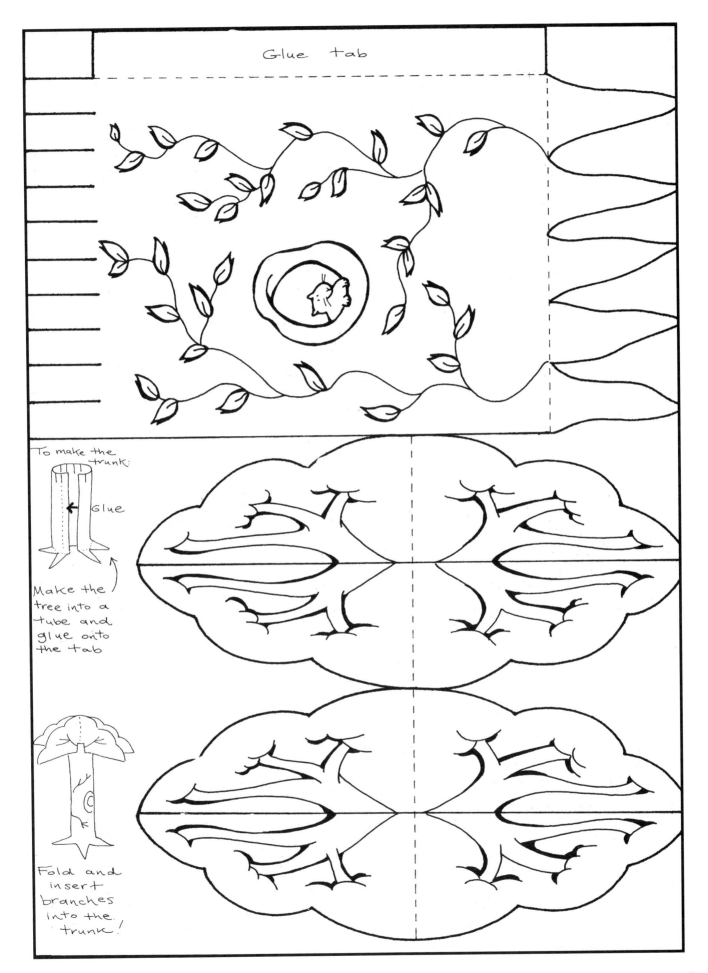

To make the trunk:

Glue

Make the tree into a tube and glue onto the tab

Fold and insert branches into the trunk!

17

Abraham and Sarah

Craft 1

Supplies: large sheet, blankets, towels, pillows, drinking straws, clay, cardboard base, plain paper towels, cold coffee, coat racks, scissors, glue, water

Houses That Moved

Let the children help you place a large sheet or blanket over coat racks to create a nomad's tent. Spread towels, blankets, and pillows on the inside. Have the children take a seat on the floor of the tent.

Say: If I had been part of Abraham's family, I would have lived in a tent instead of a house. Tents suited these people perfectly, because they raised sheep and goats and had to move a lot. When the food ran out, the people packed up their tents and moved on to another area.

Ask: What are the good things about living in a tent? What are the bad things about living in a tent? Do you think you would like to spend your entire life in a tent? (*Invite the children to comment.*)

© 2000 Abingdon Press.

Say: Imagine looking out across the land and seeing hundreds of tents. A family with many servants might have that many. They would arrange their tents in a circle for protection. The tents were made from black goat's hair and stretched about fifteen feet long and ten feet wide. The woman in a family simply added to the length of the tent as a family grew. A curtain in the center of the tent divided the tent into men's quarters and women's quarters. Furnishings of a tent were very simple. There were simple mats of straw or wool or coarse camel hair rugs. Bed rolls were stacked along the sides of the tents and were brought out at nighttime. All cooking was done outdoors.

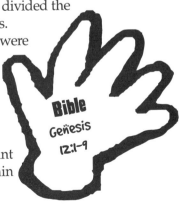

Bible
Genesis
12:1–9

Give each child nine drinking straws that have been cut to a length of six inches, a small amount of clay, a twelve-inch cardboard base, and a plain paper towel. Make clay bases for each of the

19

straws so that they will stand up. Arrange them on the cardboard base as shown in the diagram on the previous page.

Dip the paper towel into the mixture of cold coffee. Wring it out. Then dip it into the mixture of white glue and water. Wring it out. Drape the paper towel over the straws, forming a nomad's tent. Set aside to dry for the rest of the class time.

craft 2

Supplies: figures (see page 21), crayons or markers, scissors, paste or glue, wooden craft sticks, modeling clay, sand, nomad's tent (see previous craft), construction paper (optional: fabric scraps, cotton balls, needle, thread)

People of Hair Houses

Give each child a set of figures (see page 21) for the nomad's diorama. Have the children color the figures and then cut them out.

Then, using the diagram below as a guide, show the children how to fold the figures on the dotted line. Put paste or glue on the insides of both sides of the figures and center a wooden craft stick inside the figures. Leave about one-half inch of the stick extending at the base of the figures. Create bases for them from modeling clay.

Push the ends of the craft sticks into the clay. Firm the clay around the sticks so that the figures will stand up. Place the figures in and around the nomad's tent that they made in the previous craft. The children can sprinkle sand lightly around the tent area for added realism.

Then let the children create the inside things for their nomad tent diorama. Provide fabric scraps and construction paper. Children who may want to create pillows might stitch around small squares of fabric and stuff them with cotton balls.

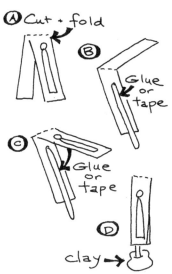

Say: At first God's people were travelers when they came to Canaan. The word we use to describe a person who lives this kind of life is "nomad." Nomads would move on when food and water ran out. Theirs was a simple life—an outdoor life. And the people always knew that God was with them. God went with them wherever they went.

20

21

Rebekah

craft

Supplies: 3-foot squares of muslin (one per child), alum, ingredients to make a natural dye, old pots, water, cream of tartar, strainer, wooden paint stirrer

Dip and Dye

Say: Women in Bible times used every opportunity to decorate their clothing with colorful embroidery and dye, since the Palestinian landscape was so drab. They wanted as much color as they could get. Dyes were made from plants that grew naturally in the environment.

Let the children experience dying simple muslin scarfs. You can use any of these natural ingredients: dandelion flowers (yellow), elderberries (violet), marigolds (yellow-tan), red onion skins (reddish orange), yellow onion skins (yellow to burnt orange). Use alum (available at a local pharmacy) as your mordant (the agent that fixes dye colors).

Fill an old pot with enough water to cover the muslin the day before you dye your fabric. Add four ounces of alum mixed with one ounce cream of tartar. Bring to a boil and cook for one hour. Let the muslin cool overnight in the mordant bath.

For a small amount of fabric you will only need a couple of handfuls of your dyestuffs for each color.

Let the children help you put the plants and a little water in another old pot. Simmer for about 30 minutes. Strain the dye. Return the dye to its pot. Add the muslin and enough cold water to cover the fabric.

Place the pot containing the dye and fabric back on the stove. Stirring the fabric around with a wooden paint stirrer, cook until the fabric is the shade you want. Let the fabric cool in the pot.

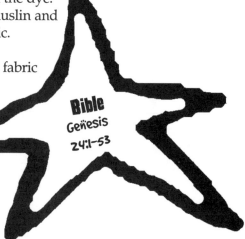

Bible
Genesis
24:1-53

Rinse in cool water. Hang to dry.

22

Jacob and Esau

Craft 1

Supplies: newspaper, paint smocks, sponges, paper plates, tempera paint, tablespoon, paper

Thumbody Special

Cover a table with newspaper. Have the children wear smocks. Put a sponge in each paper plate. Put a tablespoon of tempera paint on each sponge.

Say: Jacob and Esau were twins, but they were nothing alike. Each had his own special gifts and talents. God made us all that way. There is absolutely no one in the world who is exactly like you.

Have the children press their fingers and thumbs into paint and press them onto paper, making fingerprints. Let the children notice the differences.

© 1998 Abingdon Press.

Craft 2

Supplies: super spinner (see page 24), scissors, glue, posterboard, unsharpened pencils or quarter-inch dowels, tape

Super Spinners

Give each child a copy of the super spinner (see page 24).

Say: These super spinners have a secret message that we all need to remember. (*God loves me.*)

Have each child cut out the two circles. Glue the circles to small pieces of posterboard. Cut them out again. Tape the sides of the posterboard circles together, making sure the printed sides are facing out. Insert an unsharpened pencil or a dowel between the two posterboard circles and tape it in place. Have the children extend their arms and roll the pencils between their palms. The message will come together as *God loves me.*

Bible
Genesis
25:19-28

© 1998 Abingdon Press.

Jacob's Ladder

craft

Supplies: stairway and angel (see page 26), envelopes, glue, cotton balls, magnetic strips, construction paper or wooden craft sticks

Walking Angels

Say: Today we're hearing about a stairway that went from the earth to heaven. Going up and down that stairway were angels. Let's make this stairway to remind us that God is not somewhere far away. God is right here with us on earth. No matter where we go or what we do, God's love is always there.

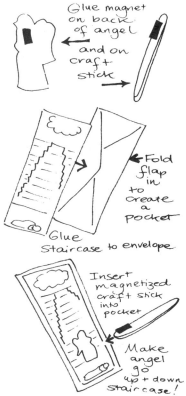

Glue magnet on back of angel and on craft stick

Fold flap in to create a pocket

Glue Staircase to envelope.

Insert magnetized craft stick into pocket

Make angel go up + down staircase!

© 1998 Abingdon Press.

Give each child the stairway and angel (see page 26). Have the children tuck the flap of the envelope inside. Glue the stairway onto the front of the envelope. Glue cotton balls at the top to represent heaven. Have the children color the stairway and the angels.

Then cut one-half inch lengths from magnetic strips, two for each child. Glue one to the back of the angels as shown here. Fold the construction paper over and over, forming an inch-wide paper stick. (You may substitute a wooden craft stick.) Glue the second magnetic strip piece to the top of the construction paper stick or craft stick. Slip the paper strip into the envelope from the side.

Hold the angel until the magnet on the strip catches the angel. Then move the angel up and down the stairway.

© 1998 Abingdon Press.

Bible
Genesis
28:10-22

Baby Moses

Craft 1

Supplies: basket, handle, and coupons (see page 29); glue or stapler and staples; scissors

Basket Full 'o Love

Say: Our families are special. God wants us to show love to our families. We can do that in many ways. Let's make a basket full of love to share.

Have the children cut out the basket, handle, and coupons (see page 29). Fold the basket on the dotted lines. Glue or staple the two sides. Glue one end of the handle to the back and one end to the front. Place the coupons in the basket. The coupons indicate the different ways the child agrees to show love to family members during the coming week.

© 1997 Abingdon Press.

Craft 2

Supplies: cardboard, scissors, puffy paint (recipe on the next page), newspaper, markers, resealable plastic bags, yarn, paper punch

By Any Other Name

Before class, cut cardboard into license-plate shaped rectangles. Make up several sets of the puffy paint. (See the recipe on the next page.)

Ask: How did Moses get his name? (*The princess gave it to him. His name means "to draw out from the water."*) Do any of you know what your names mean?

Invite the children to share the origins of their names. If you have a baby name book, look up some of their names in it and tell the children what they mean.

Bible
Exodus
2:1-10

27

Say: In Bible times names had very special uses. The name told who a person was, who his father was, or something about the person. Sometimes a person was named after another object. Just like today, names made a person special. Moses got a special name because of what happened to him at an early age. Because of what happened to him, Moses lived to be a very special person.

Cover the tables with newspaper. Give each child a cardboard rectangle. Have each child write his or her name on the cardboard, using big fat letters. With younger children you may need to assist. Make sure the letters are large and thick. Then have the children use the plastic bags to squeeze the puffy paint onto their letters. Outline the letters first. Then fill in all the empty spaces. Once the names are done, the children can decorate the remaining spaces. Set aside to dry.

When the name plaques are dry, punch holes in the top and thread yarn through them. Tie the ends together so that name plaques can be hung.

To make puffy paint: Combine 1 cup flour, 1 cup salt, and 1 cup water. Divide the mixture into four portions. Add food coloring to each portion. Put each color in a separate resealable plastic bag. Snip the corner from the bag. Squeeze the mixture through the hole.

Craft 3

Supplies: substantial paper plates, blue plastic wrap, grass seed, cotton balls, white glue, walnut shells, large wooden beads, small fabric squares, water, tape

Moses in the Reeds

Give each child a paper plate. Show the children how to cover the paper plates with blue plastic wrap. Have them secure the plastic wrap on the backs of their plates with tape. Let each child glue cotton balls around the edge of one half of his or her plate. Show the children how to spread out the cotton balls. Have the children dampen the cotton balls slightly and sprinkle grass seed over them.

Give each child a large wooden bead, a walnut shell, and a fabric square. Have each child wrap the bead with fabric and place it in the walnut shell. Tell the children to glue the walnut shells onto the plates in areas where there is blue plastic, representing water. Put the plates in a sunny location. Tell the children to keep their cotton balls damp.

Say: Very soon the grass will sprout, and you will be able to see baby Moses in his basket, floating on the water.

28

One
hug
at any time

An
extra chore
with
no griping

Ten minutes
of
quiet time

Help
on
any job

The Burning Bush

craft 1

Supplies: burning bush (see page 31), crayons or markers, scissors, paper fasteners or large snaps, paper punch

Make a Burning Bush

Give each child the burning bush (see page 31). Have the children color and cut out the picture of Moses kneeling in front of the burning bush. Have the children color the flames orange, yellow, and red. Then have them cut them out and attach them to the back of the model with a paper fastener. If you have a paper punch, punch holes in both pieces where indicated. Line up the holes and push the paper fastener through. If you do not have a paper fastener, a large snap will work just as well.

© 1998 Abingdon Press.

craft 2

Supplies: newspaper or plastic, pencils, cardboard, flour, salt, water, food coloring, large bowl, resealable plastic sandwich bags, spoons, scissors

From Bags to Bushes

Ask the students to help you cover a table with newspaper or plastic. Give each student a piece of cardboard and a pencil. Ask everyone to outline a bush on his or her piece of cardboard.

Combine 1 cup flour, 1 cup salt, and 1 cup water in a large bowl. (If you have a large class, you will need more than one recipe.) Have resealable plastic sandwich bags and food coloring where they can be easily reached and shared. Have each student spoon a small amount of the mixture into a plastic bag and add a few drops of food coloring. Encourage everyone to try to create several different colors of paint. Have the children seal the bags and knead the mixture gently. Then snip off a small corner of the bags. Have the students squeeze different colors of paint onto their pieces of cardboard to create interesting pictures of burning bushes.

Bible
Exodus
3:1-6

31

Let My People Go!

craft

Supplies: paper

Make an Origami Hopping Frog

Say: Chances are you share your life with a frog. Frogs aren't fussy about where they live, as long as the place is damp. You probably have a frog living under your porch or back steps. Let's make a hopping frog. Challenge the persons in your family or neighborhood to a hopping frog contest.

Give each child an eight-inch square of paper. (Leftover gift wrap works well.) Have the children place the paper wrong side up on the table and fold it in half, first one way and then the other. (Open to full size between these folds.)

Have the children fold each corner to the center. Crease. Have them fold points A and B so that they meet in the middle of the paper.

Following the diagram, show the children how to fold the bottom up. Have them fold A and B again so that they meet in the middle at the bottom of the paper. Have the children fold the bottom up, about one third of the way, and fold this piece down in half again. Then have them fold the top point down.

Have the children turn the frog over and press their fingers down on the frog's back. When the children slide their fingers off, watch the frogs hop away.

**Bible
Exodus
8:1-7**

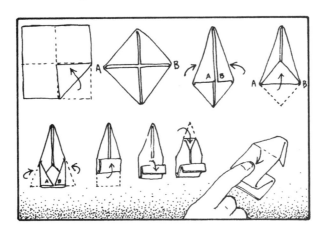

Ten Commandments

craft

Supplies: 2 cups flour, 1 cup salt, 2 cups water, 2 tablespoons of oil, 1 tablespoon of cream of tartar, toothpicks, saucepan, mixing spoon (optional: food coloring)

Make Clay Tablets

Combine all the ingredients in a saucepan. Working together, stir over low heat. Don't let the mixture stick to the pan. Keep stirring until the mixture thickens.

Remove the saucepan from the stove and let the dough cool until it is ready to handle.

Place the dough on a floured surface and knead until the dough is smooth. Form the dough into tablet shapes. Carve a rule or one of the commandments into each tablet shape with a toothpick. Allow to dry.

Option: Add food coloring to the dough to give it color.

Bible
Exodus
20:1-17

Ruth and Naomi

craft 1

Supplies: plates, scissors, crayons or markers, crepe paper, tape, stapler and staples

Love Shakers

You will need two plates for each child. Cut each paper plate in half. This will make two shakers. Then give each child four paper plate halves.

Have the children decorate the bottom sides of each half-plate with hearts and things that remind the children of love.

Cut brightly colored crepe paper into twenty-four-inch lengths. Then have the children select eight streamers (four for each shaker). Tape together the ends of each group of four. Then tape a set to the insides of two of the paper plate halves. Let the streamers extend over the curved sides of the plates.

Place a second paper plate on top of the first of each set (inside surfaces together). Staple around the curved edges, leaving the straight edges free. Show the children how to slip their hands inside the openings.

© 1999 Abingdon Press.

craft 2

Supplies: love lights picture (see page 36), tape, black construction paper; push pins, sharpened pencils, or toothpicks

Love Lights

Say: When we follow Jesus, we can't help but love one another. This love shows all over us. It shines like a light from inside of us.

Give each child a copy of the love lights picture (see page 36). Tape the picture

Bible
Ruth
1–4

to a sheet of black construction paper so that it will not slip as the children are punching the design. Then let the children punch out the design using the push pins, sharpened pencils, or toothpicks. Caution them not to miss a single dot.

When the children are finished, let them hold the picture up to the window or to a light. The design will shine through.

craft 3

Supplies: red or pink construction paper, scissors, pens, white glue, spring-type clothespins

Love Notes

Cut heart shapes from construction paper. On each heart write something you will do for someone else to show your love for him or her. Glue the heart onto a spring clothespin. Attach the clothespins where that person can find them.

craft 4

Supplies: plaster of Paris, mixing bowl, plastic spoons, plastic knives, pin backs, metallic glitter, spray gloss varnish, white glue

Love Casts

Mix the plaster of Paris according to package instructions. Fill a plastic spoon with the plaster and smooth the top with a knife so that the plaster is level with the edge of the spoon.

Press a pin back into the plaster. Let the plaster harden for at least an hour. Pop the plaster shapes out of the spoons.

Coat the plaster shape with white glue. Sprinkle the metallic glitter over the shapes, and spray with the varnish when dry.

Say: You can share these special pins with friends that you love.

David and Goliath

craft

Supplies: cardboard, heavy-duty scissors or a craft knife, aluminum foil, masking tape, white glue, string, newspaper, pencils

Make a Family Shield

Cut a shield shape out of cardboard. Tell the children to make designs on the shield that represent their families. Have the children draw the designs on the cardboard with a pencil.

Show the children how to dip strings in white glue and lay them on the outline of the design and any interior lines they want to show.

When the shields are dry, have the children cover them with aluminum foil, pressing close around the string so that it will show through. Have the children tape the aluminum foil down on the back.

Bible
I Samuel
17:1-50

David and Jonathan

craft

Supplies: safety pins and small colored beads (option: neon shoelaces)

Make Friendship Pins

Have the children thread colored glass beads onto the straight bar of a safety pin. Encourage them to make special designs and give the pins to friends.

Let the children make friendship necklaces by threading the round hole at the base of the safety pin onto a neon-colored shoelace. Let each create his or her own design.

   Say: You can collect friendship pins from all your friends.

Bible
1 Samuel
18:1-4

David and Abigail

craft

Supplies: dove and heart patterns (see page 40), lightweight cardboard, scissors, marker, white paper plates, glue, construction paper, paper punch, yarn, tape

Peace and Love

Photocopy of the dove and heart patterns (see page 40) for each child. Except for the heart with the Bible verse, re-trace the patterns onto lightweight cardboard (such as old file folders). Use the patterns to cut multiple doves and hearts for the project. You will need approximately four to six doves and ten hearts in a variety of sizes per child.

Say: Today we're talking about a young woman named Abigail. In Bible times women were not considered to be equal to men. They were thought of as property in many cases. But Abigail solved a problem early, before it could become a much bigger problem. She stepped in and kept one person from doing something he would have regretted. Abigail did not cause the problem; however, she stepped in to find the solution to the problem. Sometimes we are called to step in to be peacemakers. We may not have caused the problem, but we can sometimes help people stop the conflict.

Have the children cut out the centers of white paper plates, leaving the outside rims of the plates. Using the patterns, cut out doves and hearts. Then using the diagram on the next page as a guide, let the children glue the doves and hearts around the outsides of the plates.

When the entire rims of the plates are covered, let each child cut out a Bible verse heart. Punch a hole in the top of each heart and thread a length of yarn through the hole. Adjust the yarn so that the heart hangs down in the center of the plate when taped in place. Then attach another piece of yarn to each plate to make a hanger.

Bible
1 Samuel
25:2–35

Blessed are the peacemakers, for they will be called children of God. (Matthew 5:9)

punch out

Cut out center of paper plate

Glue on doves and hearts

BACK OF WREATH

Back of Bible verse heart

Thread Bible Verse heart with Yarn. Tape to back of wreath.

Solomon's Temple

CRAFT 1

Supplies: empty tin cans, metal file, water, permanent marker, hammer, nail, newspaper, votive candles or tea light candles, long matches, paper, tape, pens

Praise God Lamps

Say: Let's create a lamp to remind us to praise God every day in every way.

Before class begins, rinse and remove the labels from tin cans. File down any sharp edges. Fill the cans with water to within a half-inch of the top and place them in the freezer overnight.

Tell the children to think about the design they want on their lamp. Have them draw the design first on a template. Have them tape the template to their cans.

Have each child hold his or her can. Place it on several thicknesses of newspaper and punch out the design by placing a nail on the line of the design and tapping it lighting until the nail goes through the can. Continue making nail holes all along the design.

Set the can in a sink filled with warm water. Dry the can when the ice falls out, and place the votive candles or tealight candles inside.

Hint: You may want to have additional adult assistance for this activity.

Bible
1 Kings
6:1-14

craft 2

Supplies: plastic container, measuring cups and spoons, 4 tablespoons cellulose wallpaper paste, 4 cups cold water, mixing spoon, old plastic tablecloth or drop cloth, newspapers, ruler, bowls to use as molds, wax paper, paper towels, salad oil, plastic wrap, scissors, gesso sealer, acrylic paints, paintbrushes of assorted sizes, clear acrylic spray

Bowl Me Over

In the plastic container mix the wallpaper paste with the cold water. Have the children take turns stirring the mixture. Let it sit for at least fifteen minutes, then have them stir again.

Cover the work surface with the tablecloth or drop cloth. Tear newspapers into strips about one inch by five inches long.

Let each child turn the bowl she or he will use as a mold upside down on wax paper. Have the child use a paper towel to rub the outside of the bowl with salad oil then cover the outside of the bowl with plastic wrap.

Show the children how to dip strips of newspaper into the wallpaper paste. Have them run the strips through their fingers to remove any excess paste. Then have them lay the strips over the bottoms of their bowls. Tell the children to continue laying pasted strips on the bowls until the bowls are totally covered.

Let the bowls dry on wax paper for a day or so. Put at least five more coats of pasted newspaper strips on each large bowl and two or three more coats on each small bowl. Let each coat dry completely before starting the next.

During the next class period have the children carefully remove the paper bowls from the mold bowls. Tell them to remove the plastic wrap. Let them use scissors to cut the edges of their bowls as desired—straight, pointed, wavy, and so forth. Help each child place one more layer of newspaper on the rim of the bowl and anywhere the bowl feels thin.

Let the children paint the bowls with gesso sealer. Let that coat dry for ten to fifteen minutes and then apply a second coat. Let it dry. Then have the children decorate the bowls with acrylic paints. Once the paint dries, help each child spray his or her bowl with two coats of clear acrylic coating. Allow the bowls to dry between coats.

Hint: These bowls are for dry food only. Do not put them in the dishwasher. Clean them with a damp sponge.

Josiah Finds the Scrolls

craft

Supplies: brown wrapping paper, scissors, plastic dishpan, water, newspaper, ironing board and iron, examples of illuminated manuscripts, permanent felt-tip markers or crayons, large piece of paper, yarn

Pictured Parchments

Cut brown wrapping paper into pieces about twenty-two inches wide by twelve inches high. Place a plastic dishpan partially filled with water on a table covered with newspaper. Set up an ironing board and iron away from traffic areas. Use adult supervision.

Bring in examples of illuminated manuscripts from medieval times. (Libraries are good sources for these.) Put the manuscripts where the children can look at them. Point out that the people who made these illustrations wanted readers to know how special and important she or he thought the words were.

Ask: What are some things the Bible tells us we can do to be faithful to God? (*Write these down on a large sheet of paper. Do not make a lengthy list, but write enough that the children will have several ways in which they can be faithful to choose from.*)

Say: Today we are going to make illuminated scrolls to take home to remind us what we can do to be faithful to God. Choose one or more of these things and write it on the scroll. Then illustrate the manuscript just as the scribes and monks did so long ago.

Have the children do the writing and illustrating with permanent markers or crayons. Crumple the scroll into a ball and dip it in water. Squeeze the water out and open the scroll carefully. Place the opened scroll between two sheets of newspaper. Iron until dry. Roll into a scroll. Tie with yarn.

Say: The words of the Bible help us to know how to be faithful to God.

Bible
2 kings
22:8–23:3

House of the Lord

craft

Supplies: newspaper, masking tape

Newspaper Rods

Make life-sized structures. Four or five children can work together on their structure. While two people build, three can roll newspaper tubes.

Place two pieces of newspaper on the floor. Sit at the point of one corner. Fold the corner to the center fold.

Beginning at the straight edge roll the newspaper as tightly as possible into a tube. Tape the corner so that it won't unroll.

Use masking tape to connect rods. The children may find it easiest to tape three rods together in the form of a triangle and connect triangles to form geodesic domes or structures of any shape they can imagine. Encourage creativity!

The more tightly rolled the newspaper rods, the stronger and sturdier the structure.

Bible
Psalm
122:1

Jeremiah

Craft

Supplies: Jeremiah story figures (see page 46), business-size envelopes, crayons or markers, scissors, glue or stapler and staples, yarn, tape

Get Out of the Well!

Give each child a copy of the Jeremiah action figure, the two friends, and the well (see page 46). Let the children color the individual pieces.

Let each child cut out the pieces he or she has colored and the fitting (the narrow strip with three dotted lines). Show the child how to cut the slit in the dry well wall that will allow Jeremiah to be pulled from the well. Let each child glue the picture of Jeremiah's friends to the top of the well.

Glue or staple the edges of the well wall onto a business-size envelope, making sure not to glue the center of the well wall. Then fold the fitting on the dotted lines (see the diagram below). Attach the fitting to the back of the Jeremiah figure and slip it into the open slit in the well. Make sure the fitting is between the well wall and the envelope.

1 Tape strip to back of Jeremiah

2 Slip one side of strip behind slit in well, then the other. Back of Well

3 Thread yarn as shown & in tends. Staple friends to top of well.

4 Staple assembled Well to envelope.

Punch the holes where indicated on Jeremiah and on the picture of Jeremiah's friends. Attach the yarn around Jeremiah with both ends extending to the top of the well. Thread the ends through the holes on the picture of the two friends. Tie the ends together. As you pull the yarn, Jeremiah will be pulled from the well.

Ask: How did Jeremiah find himself in the dry well? (*He wouldn't keep from telling the people what God expected them to do.*) What do we learn about sharing the good news from Jeremiah? (*It isn't always easy to tell other people about God and about what God wants them to do.*)

Bible
Jeremiah
38:6-13

Attach piece with friends here ➘

friends ⬆

Jeremiah ⬇

FITTING

Daniel and the Lions

Craft 1

Supplies: lion puppet (see page 49), scissors, crayons or markers, cardboard, glue, drawing paper

Make Lion Puppets

Photocopy one lion puppet (see page 49) for each child.

Let each child color, cut out, and assemble the lion puppet according to the directions. Let the children add small bits of cardboard to the back of each piece before gluing it to the base. This makes the puppet three-dimensional. Fold a piece of drawing paper over and over. Use this as the base for the puppet. Let the children put their names on the completed puppets.

Have the children stand in a line, one behind the other. Ask them to hold up their lion puppets. Use these motions with the rhyme: hop up and extend right foot. Hop up and bring the right foot to its original position. Repeat. Use the same actions for the left foot. Hop forward. Hop backward. Hop forward three hops (on the roar, roar, roar). Repeat for each verse of the poem.

The teacher should say the first three lines; the children will repeat the fourth line as they hop forward.

> In a land so far away,
> There lived a man who liked to pray,
> Prayed to God three times a day.
> **Roar, roar, roar.**
>
> Some jealous men dreamed up a plan,
> And sent a law throughout the land,
> Decreeing prayers to God were banned.
> **Roar, roar, roar.**
>
> But Daniel chose to do what's right
> And in his room within plain sight,
> He prayed to God both day and night.
> **Roar, roar, roar.**

Bible
Daniel
6:10-23

Daniel was the king's good friend,
But still was put into the den,
Because of other jealous men.
Roar, roar, roar.

With lions Daniel spent the night.
The king rushed down at morning's light,
To find that Daniel was all right!
Roar, roar, roar.

© 1997 Abingdon Press.

craft 2

Supplies: oatmeal box, string, construction paper, scissors, tape, glue, paper clips

Make a Roaring Lion

Poke a hole in the top of an oatmeal box. Thread a twelve-inch piece of string through the hole. Tie a large knot on the inside of the lid so that the string will not pull through. (You might want to tie a paper clip to the string to ensure this.)

Help the children cover the box with brown construction paper. Have them tape the cover onto the box. Have the children cut out two circles each, one about the size of the end of the oatmeal box, the other about four inches larger. Tell them to draw a lion face on the smaller circle and glue the lion face in the center of the larger circle. Show the children how to make cuts from the edge of the larger circle to the smaller circle. This is the lion's mane. Let the children glue the lion's mane onto the oatmeal box.

Show the children how to make the lions roar by grasping the string between their thumbnails and second fingers. Have them drag your nails along the string.

Say: Listen to the lion roar.

© 1997 Abingdon Press.

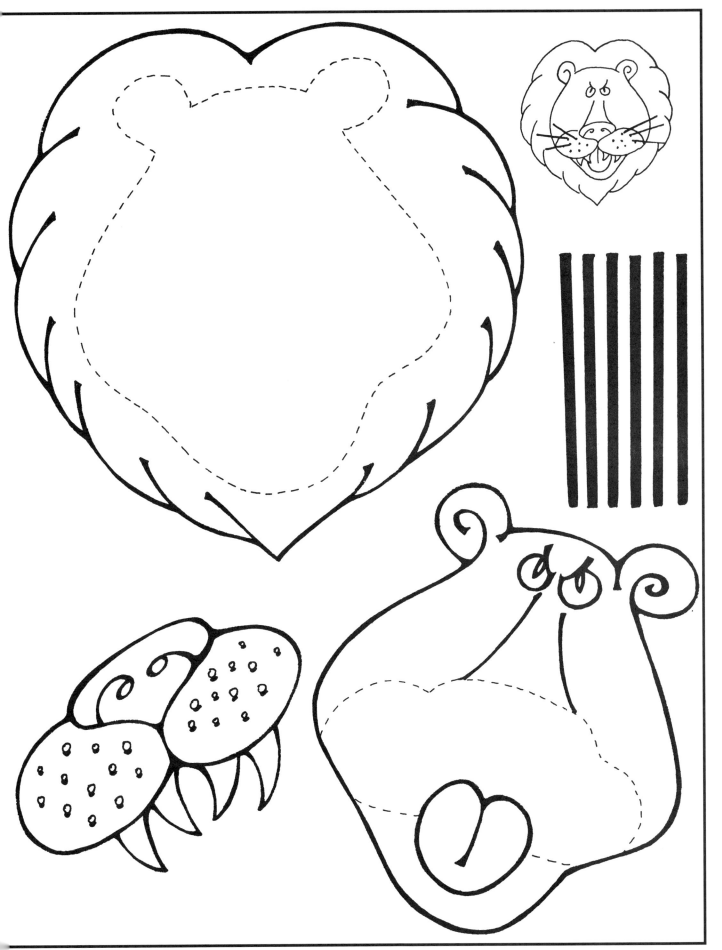

Amos

craft

Supplies: light switchplates, newspaper, white glue, water, bowl, paintbrushes; decorating items such as stickers, decals, ribbons, rickrack, acrylic paints, fabric scraps, wrapping paper

Do—Right Lights

Give each child a plastic switchplate and a variety of decorating supplies. Cover the tables with recycled newspaper. For a final touch, dilute white glue with water and let the children paint over their creations.

Say: Amos called the people to turn away from evil and do what was right. Let's make a reminder to ourselves to always try to do what we know is right. When we put this reminder in our rooms, we will be reminded to do what is right every day as we go in and out.

Let the children decorate their switchplates. They can use stickers, decals, ribbons, rickrack, acrylic paints, fabric scraps, and wrapping paper. Allow the switchplates to dry. Remind the children to ask an adult to remove their switchplates from the wall at home and to put the ones they made in their place.

© 1999 Abingdon Press.

Bible
Amos
5:14

Jonah and the Big Fish

Craft 1

Supplies: name fish (see page 53), crayons or markers, scissors, stapler and staples, cotton balls or tissue paper, paper clips

Go Fishing!

Have the children create name fish (see page 53). Have them decorate both sides of the fish and write their names somewhere on it. Then let the children cut out the fish and staple around the edges, leaving the top open. Stuff the fish lightly with cotton balls or tissue paper. Staple the hole and attach a paper clip to the top fin.

Say: Today we're talking about a man named Jonah. He learns a very important message: God's love is for everyone. Does that mean you? or you? or you? (*Point to each of the children in turn.*)

Say: Of course it does!

Craft 2

Supplies: "Who Swallowed Jonah?" (see page 54), crayons or markers, scissors, tape or stapler and staples, rubber bands

Who Swallowed Jonah?

Give each child "Who Swallowed Jonah?" (see page 54). The children will color the fish and Jonah. Have them cut out the figures. Fold both on the dotted lines.

Tape and/or staple one end of a rubber band inside Jonah. The remainder of the rubber band will hang out the foot end

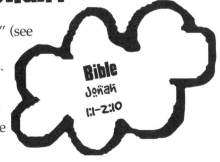

Bible
Jonah
1:1-2:10

about two inches. Staple around the three open sides of the figure, and where the rubber band is taped. Place Jonah inside the folded fish so that only the tip of the head is showing through the fish's mouth.

Open the fish. Extend the rubber band without stretching and tape and/or staple the end down. Staple around the the open edges of the fish. Staple through all thicknesses, catching the taped rubber band.

Hold the fish where your fingers are also on the taped end of the rubber band. Gently pull Jonah from the mouth of the fish. Then let go. Jonah will pop back in.

> **Ask:** When you pull Jonah out of the fish, what is he holding? (*a heart*) What does the heart say? (*God's love is for everyone.*)

Craft 3

Supplies: three-dimensional fabric paint (red, pink, white), and plastic sandwich bags

Make a God's Love Magnet

Have the children place their sandwich bags on a flat surface. Show them how to outline a heart with the fabric paint. Encourage them to fill in their hearts so that there are no air spaces.

Allow the hearts to dry. Show the children how to peel their hearts from the plastic bags and place them on the refrigerator or on metal surfaces. They will stick automatically.

> **Say:** Every time you see the heart, say out loud, "God's love is for everyone."

53

God's love is for everyone

NEW TESTAMENT

The Wise Men's Visit

Craft 1

Supplies: mixing bowl, measuring cup, food coloring, spoon, glue, acrylic varnish, paintbrushes, flour, salt, water, small dishes, scissors, small cardboard boxes, construction paper, pencil, plastic squeeze bottles (like ketchup servers)

Puffy Top Gift Boxes

To make puffy paints, mix one cup flour, one cup water, and one cup salt. Divide evenly into small dishes. Add food coloring to each dish to make a different color. Let the children help you create new and different colors.

Have the children turn the tops of the boxes to be covered upside down on the paper. Have the children draw around the edges. Let them cut out the paper and glue it to the tops of the boxes. Have the children draw simple designs on the tops of the boxes with pencils and fill in the designs with puffy paint. Let the creations dry overnight. Have each child brush on a coat of acrylic varnish to protect the work and to make it shiny. Let that dry.

Say: Decide who will get the gift. You can fill your box with special treasures, notes, or anything else you think that person will enjoy.

© 1997 Abingdon Press.

Craft 2

Supplies: dark construction paper; pencils; light-colored crayons; Epsom salts; water; small bowl; spoon; newspaper; pastry brushes, foam paintbrushes, or cotton balls (optional: hair dryer or small electric fan)

All That Glitters

Say: The star has come to represent for Christians the birth of the baby Jesus and the visit from the magi. The people who heard this story about Jesus knew that God sent Jesus to everyone, not just to the Jewish people, because the magi were from a foreign country and probably were not Jewish. God sent Jesus to be the Savior of all people everywhere.

Bible
Matthew
2:1-11

Give each child a piece of dark construction paper (black, dark blue, dark red, or dark green). Have the children draw stars with a pencil or create a template and let them trace the stars. Color each of the stars with a light-colored crayon. Remind the children to color hard so that the crayon will cover all the paper in the star design.

Have the children write with a light crayon: "Jesus is the light." Remind them to bear down so that the crayon markings are thick. Recall with the children the fact that the wise men or magi watched the sky for signs. The new star was a special sign.

Mix equal parts Epsom salts and water in a small bowl. Stir until the mixture dissolves. Cover the tables with newspaper. Let the children take a pastry brush, foam paintbrush, or cotton ball and dip it into the mixture. Rub the mixture over the picture. Allow to dry. You might want to use a hair dryer or small electric fan to speed up the drying process if the children want to take the pictures home today. Anchor the papers before blowing, however. Watch ice crystals appear.

© 1999 Abingdon Press.

Supplies: pencil, white paper, scissors, lightweight cardboard, Super Sculpey modeling compound (makes six candleholders), wax paper, tape, cutting board, plastic knives, screw-off bottle caps, paintbrushes, acrylic paints, candles (base similar in size to bottle caps), glass baking dish

Starlight Candleholders

Before class begins, draw a five-inch star on a piece of white paper. Cut it out and use it as a pattern to trace stars onto cardboard. Cut out the cardboard stars. Divide the modeling compound among the children. Have them knead each piece for one minute. Tape a piece of wax paper to a cutting board. Have the children roll out their pieces of modeling compound to a thickness of about ¼ inch. Have them put cardboard stars on top of the modeling compound.

Show the children how to use small plastic knives to cut around the outside edges of their stars. Have them press bottle caps into the centers of the stars until the edges of the caps are even with the surface of the star. Let the children make as many stars as they would like.

Bake the stars in the oven in a glass baking dish. (This should be with adult supervision only.) Follow the directions on the modeling compound box for temperature directions. Have an adult remove the stars when they are done. Let the children paint their candleholders, starting with the bottoms.

© 1999 Abingdon Press.

The Beatitudes

Craft 1

Supplies: plain white ceramic mugs, Liquitex Glossies Acrylic Enamels paint (found at most craft stores), newspaper, plastic plate, small paint-brushes, damp cloth, cookie sheet, potholders, dish detergent, water

Marvelous Mugs

Before class begins, wash the mugs with dish detergent and water. Dry them completely.

Cover the work surface with newspaper. Shake the paint bottles. Have the children squeeze a small amount of paint on a plate. Let them paint designs on the sides of their mugs with a medium-thick coat of paint. On the other side of their mugs, have them write one of Jesus' teachings that they want to remember. Tell them to start over if they make a mistake; they can wipe the paint off with a damp rag.

The paints are non-toxic, but still encourage the children not to paint the inside of the mugs or anything else that comes in contact with food or drink.

When the children finish painting, have them clean their brushes with water. Set the mugs aside to dry for at least six hours.

Preheat an oven to 325 degrees. Place the painted mugs on the cookie sheet. Have an adult put the sheet on the middle rack of the oven. Bake for 40 minutes. Run the oven fan to keep the kitchen well-ventilated.

Have an adult remove the cookie sheet from the oven. Let the mugs cool completely before you handle them.

58

Bible
Matthew
5:3-12

Craft 2

Supplies: "words to the wise" (see page 60), lunch-sized paper bags, triangles (two small, one large per child), newspaper, rubber bands, yellow and brown construction paper, scissors, glue

Words to the Wise

Make a copy of the "words to the wise" (see page 60) for each child. From brown construction paper cut two small triangles and one large triangle for each owl. (The bases of the two small triangles should be the same width as the small ends of the bottoms of the paper bags. The bases of the large triangles should be the same width as the long sides of the bottoms of the paper bags.)

Ask: Did your mom or dad or anyone else give you any good words of advice before you came here today? What did the person say? (*Invite the children to share. Share with them some of the good advice that you give to your own family if they have a hard time getting started.*) Can you think of any other time when people have given you good advice? (*Invite the children to share those words of wisdom.*)

Say: Jesus gave people good advice. If the people followed this good advice, they would be truly happy. All it took was for people to adjust their attitudes from thinking only of ME, ME, ME to thinking about others.

Continue: Today we are going to make Words to the Wise Owls. On our owls we are going to attach some of the words of wisdom that Jesus gave to the people.

Have the children stuff the bags with the newspaper. Gather the ends of the bags and secure with rubber bands. Turn the bags upside down, so that the gathered parts are on the bottom. Glue the two small triangles and the large triangle on each bag as shown here. Cut two large circles for each bag from the yellow construction paper to be the eyes. Encourage the children to cut out the "words to the wise" cards and separate the positive "words to the wise" from the negative terms. Then let the children glue the "words to the wise" onto the bodies of their owls. Tell the children to set the owls in their rooms at home to remind them of what Jesus taught.

59

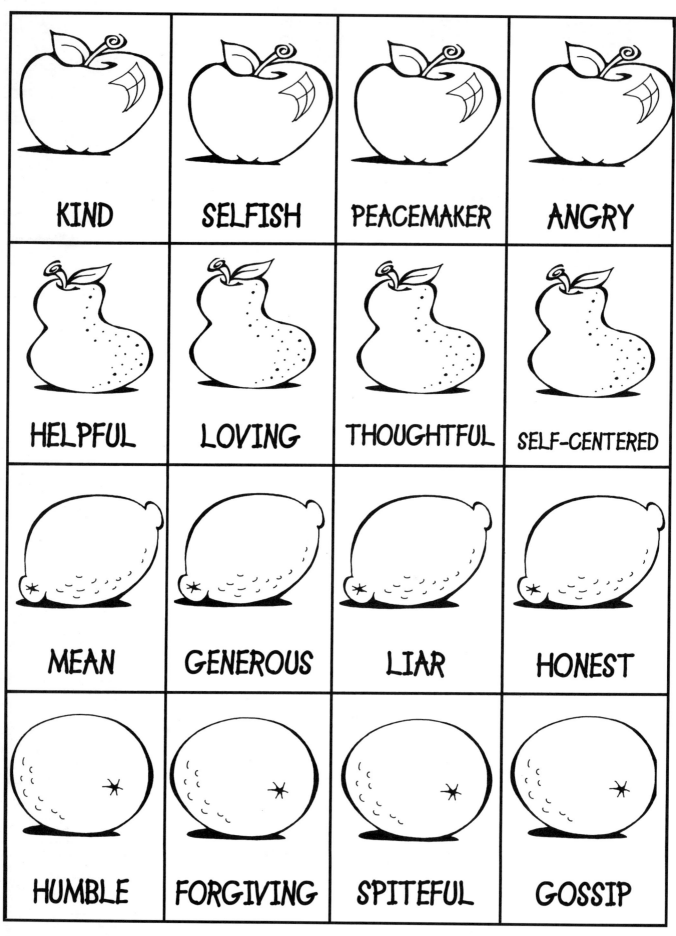

KIND   SELFISH   PEACEMAKER   ANGRY

HELPFUL   LOVING   THOUGHTFUL   SELF-CENTERED

MEAN   GENEROUS   LIAR   HONEST

HUMBLE   FORGIVING   SPITEFUL   GOSSIP

The Centurion's Servant

craft

Supplies: cardboard, scissors, pencils, string, white glue, heavy-duty aluminum foil, black shoe polish, masking tape, paintbrushes, smocks

Make a Roman Shield

Cut large circles from cardboard. Have the children use pencils to make a design on the outsides of their shields. Encourage the children to choose a design that represents something their family does or likes.

Cut the string into smaller lengths about twelve to eighteen inches long so that they are easier to handle. Have the children trace the pencil lines with white glue. Show them how to lay the string over the glue. Allow the shields to dry.

Cut a piece of heavy-duty aluminum foil large enough to cover the front of the shield and to wrap around to the back about two to three inches. Help the children press the aluminum foil over the string and press around the design. Then mix a little white glue with black shoe polish. Let the children paint over the fronts of their shields and allow to dry.

Make handles from cardboard so that one handle can be attached to each shield with masking tape. Show the children how to slip their hands into it and hold their shields.

Remind your child that the Romans were technically the enemies of the Hebrew people. They were the conquerors of their land. But Jesus took time to heal the servant of the centurion because of the centurion's great faith.

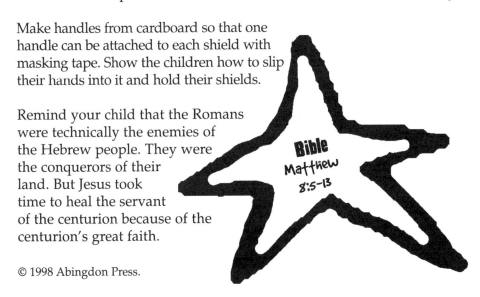

Bible
Matthew
8:5-13

61

The Lost Sheep

craft

Supplies: white paper, black marker, wax paper, yarn, small bowl, white glue, water, newspaper, ribbon

Make a Curly Sheep Hanging

On a plain sheet of white paper, draw the outline of a sheep. Go over the outline with a black marker. Place a piece of wax paper over the outline. The outline of the sheep should show through.

Place a ball of yarn in a glass or a small bowl of white glue and water (mixed half and half). Soak until the yarn is thoroughly wet. Cover the work surface with newspaper.

Begin at the back of the sheep and place a line of yarn over the outline of the sheep. When you get all the way around the sheep, begin a second line of yarn just inside the first line of yarn. Continue until the sheep is filled in.

Make sure each line of yarn is right next to the line before. Do not leave large gaps. (If you want to get adventurous, create curlicues and other designs inside the sheep once the first few lines are established.

Allow the design to dry. When completely dry, peel the sheep from the wax paper. Attach a ribbon and hang in your room to remind you that God loves and cares about you.

© 1998 Abingdon Press.

Bible
Matthew
18:10-14

The Unforgiving Servant

craft

Supplies: Bible verse reminder (see page 64), envelopes, scissors, glue

BV Reminder

Make a copy of the Bible verse reminder (see page 64) for each child in the class.

Say: Sometimes it is easy to forgive. Sometimes it is hard to forgive. But if we expect God to forgive us for our wrongs, then we must forgive those who mistreat us.

Have the children lick the flaps on the envelopes and seal them. Then show the children how to fold the envelopes in half. Fold up one inch on either end to act as feet to hold the envelopes upright. (See the illustration on the next page.)

Cut out the figures of the puppy. Glue the heads, the tails, and the paws onto the envelopes as shown in the directions. Then cut out the Bible verse reminders. Place them on the easel and put the puppy dog paws over them, holding them in place.

Say: Place this reminder in your room at home or somewhere where you will always see it. It will remind you that you are expected to forgive others, just as God forgives you.

© 1999 Abingdon Press.

Bible
Matthew
18:23-34

You
must
forgive
one
another.

Colossians 3:13, *Good News Bible*

Glue head, paws, and tail to back of stand

Just as the Lord has forgiven you, so you also must forgive.

Glue on Bible Verse

glue

glue glue

glue

SPOT

SPOT

The Great Commission

craft

Supplies: "All People Everywhere" page (see page 66), crayons or markers, scissors, tape or glue

Jesus for All

Say: When Jesus told his friends he wanted them to tell his story to all people everywhere and to make them his disciples, he meant people all over the world. The whole world was "smaller" in Bible times—not geographically smaller, but populated with fewer people and with fewer places the disciples could actually travel to. With today's modern technology we can reach all people everywhere.

Teach the children the different ways to say: "Jesus loves me." Remind the children that believing in Jesus and being Christians are not just for our country or our people, but for all people everywhere.

Give each child a copy of "All People Everywhere" (see page 66). Let the children color the picture and with a little assistance, cut the windows in the globe. Cut apart the language squares and let the children tape or paste the squares behind each window. Point out that each square says, "Jesus loves me."

Ask: To whom can we tell the stories of Jesus? (*everyone*) Jesus' message is for all people everywhere.

Bible
Matthew
28:16-20

All People Everywhere!

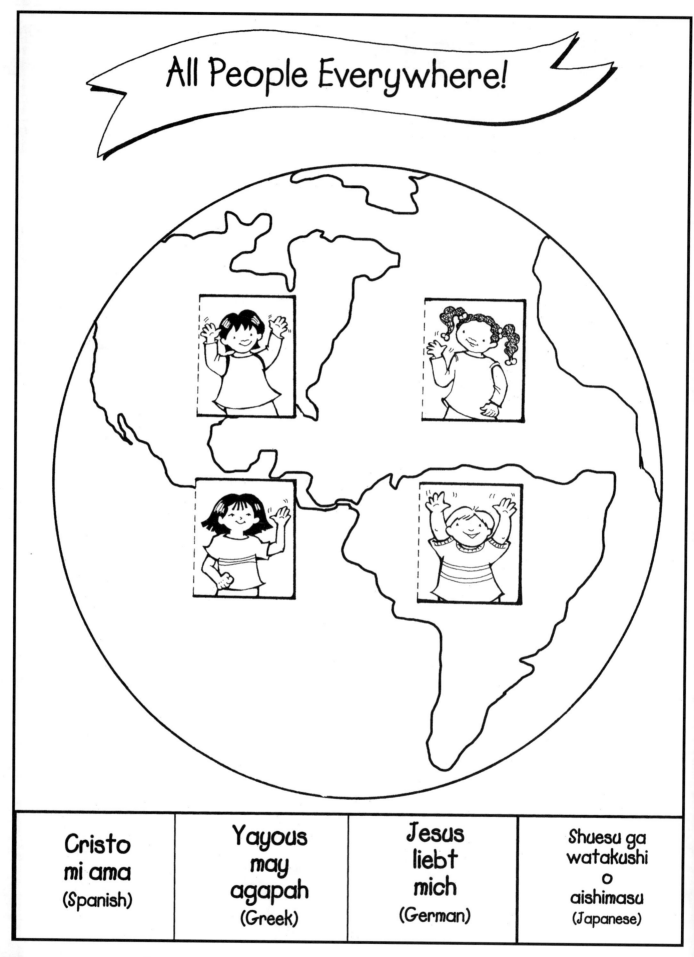

Cristo mi ama (Spanish)	Yayous may agapah (Greek)	Jesus liebt mich (German)	Shuesu ga watakushi o aishimasu (Japanese)

Jesus Calls Fishermen

Craft 1

Supplies: picture book or encyclopedia showing all kinds of fish, pencil, posterboard, scissors, newspapers, poster paint or broad-tipped felt-tip markers, paintbrushes, plastic plates or bowls for the paint, heavy duty stapler and staples

Fish Headdresses

Make a spectacular presentation of discipleship. Let each boy and girl decide which kind of fish he or she would like to be. Look through different books to get ideas.

Have the children use pencils to draw an outline of the whole fish on a piece of posterboard. Have them make the fish as large as possible. Cut out each fish. Have the children trace around this fish on a second piece of posterboard. Cut out the second fish.

Cover the table with newspapers. Have the children paint or color the outsides of their fish. Let them dry. Tell the children that they don't have to look exactly like a real fish. Encourage them to use their imaginations.

Help them staple the outer edges of the two sides together all the way around, except for the bottoms. This is where the children's heads will go.

Have the children put on their headdresses. Help them pinch the bottoms of the fish together in front of their foreheads and behind their heads.

Staple the fish together in these two spots so the headdresses fit snugly. Staple a few more times for good measure.

Bible
Mark
1:16-20

craft 2

Supplies: plastic fish (available in most toy stores), modeling compound (commercial brands such as Sculpey or Crayola), petroleum jelly, acrylic paints, paintbrushes, baking tray

Fish Plaques

Say: The fish is a reminder of the disciples who followed Jesus. Let's make a fish plaque for your home to identify yourselves as followers of Jesus.

Have the children roll out a ball of the modeling compound large enough to accommodate the size of your fish. Have them flatten the compound until it is about one-half inch thick.

Coat one side of the plastic fish with petroleum jelly. Let the children press that side of the fish into the modeling compound. Remove.

Allow the compound to dry, or bake it according to the directions on the package. When the fish plaques are dry and cool, have the children paint them with acrylic paints.

Jesus Calms the Storm

Craft

Supplies: shoeboxes, magazines or old children's resources, scissors, white glue, wrapping paper, tape, paper, marker

Make a Scary Box

Give each child a shoebox. Let the children cover the shoebox with wrapping paper.

Have magazines or old children's resources on hand. Have the children choose and cut out pictures of words or objects that express their fears. On the inside put a piece of paper with the Bible verse: "Peace! Be still!"

Show the children how to tape or glue the verse to the bottom of the box so that it is visible whenever they lift the lid.

Say: Every night when you say your prayers, open the box and read the Bible verse. Keep the box near your bed to remind yourself that God is always there.

© 1997 Abingdon Press.

Bible
Mark
4:35-41

Bartimaeus

craft

Supplies: love-colored glasses (see page 71), scissors, crayons or markers, tape or stapler and staples (optional: construction paper)

Love—colored Glasses

Say: When Jesus looked at people, he looked at them through different eyes than we do. Jesus looked at them through eyes filled with love and compassion. He did not see their disabilities. He did not see their sins. He did not see anything at all but the person inside. He recognized the potential that people had. He cared about them.

Say: Let's make love-colored glasses (see page 71) that we can use to help us see other people in better ways.

Give each child a set of the glasses. Show the children how to cut out the two pieces, attach the back piece to one side of the front piece, and adjust to fit each head.

If a child's head is bigger than the two pieces put together, extend with a piece of construction paper on each side. Before putting the final adjustment together, let the children color the glasses. Cut out the centers of the glasses. (This may require adult assistance.)

© 1997 Abingdon Press.

Bible
Mark
10:46-52

As I have loved you, so you must love one another. John 13:34

Attach back band here

Cut out

Cut out

Cut out

Attach back band here

Garden of Gethsemane

craft

Supplies: puppet (see page 73), scissors, two wooden craft sticks, white glue, tape, construction paper, stapler and staples, crayons or other decorative items (optional: lightweight posterboard)

Sleepyhead Puppet

Say: We are talking today about a time when Jesus turned to God for help. Jesus had asked his friends to help, but instead of being helpers, they were sleepyheads and kept falling asleep. Let's make sleepyhead puppets.

Give each child a puppet (see page 73). To make sure the puppet stands up, you may want to have the children glue the face onto a piece of lightweight posterboard before beginning any of the rest of the cuts.

Have the children cut out the puppet faces and eyelids on the solid lines only. Fold back the eyelids on the dotted lines. (This may need adult supervision.) Let the children color or decorate the faces.

Let each child put a drop of glue on the underside of each eyelid and place the tip end of each wooden craft stick there. While the glue is still damp, have the child shift the ends of the two craft sticks together. Tape or glue the ends of the two craft sticks together.

Help each child glue the separate eyes over the top half of the eyelid on the puppet face where the wooden craft stick was glued. Align the separate eyes directly over the eyelids on the puppet face so that they will not drag as the eyes open and close. Allow the figures to dry.

Have each child fold a piece of construction paper over and over. Staple along the loose edge and then staple to the sleepyhead puppet face to be a handle.

Let the children practice opening and shutting the eyes of the puppets.

Bible
Mark
14:32-42

72

1.

Glue

2.

Glue

tape

3.

open!

closed

Easter

craft 1

Supplies: drawing paper, crayons, paper clips

Scratch It Out

Give each child a piece of drawing paper. Set out the crayons.

Say: You may find it hard to understand why the cross is the chief symbol of our church. But the cross reminds us of a very sad time. Jesus died on the cross.

Ask: So why do you think we put the cross in our church? God raised Jesus from the dead. We are sorry Jesus died on the cross. Jesus died because he wanted to show his friends how much God loved them. The cross helps us remember this.

Have the children color the drawing paper heavily with bright colors. Then color over the bright colors with black crayon. Make it very thick.

Say: When Jesus died, the sky turned dark as night. But something wonderful was about to happen.

Show the children how to scratch out a cross design using the partially opened paper clip.

Say: Through the dark times there comes brightness. Even though Jesus was dead, it wasn't the end.

Bible
Mark
16:1-6

craft 2

Supplies: small flat sponges, tempera paint or printing ink, paper plates, paper, scissors, newspaper, water

Springy Sponge Prints

Before class begins, cut the sponges into a variety of shapes for spring, such as flowers, leaves, stems, and a sun. (A variety of shapes may be available in your local craft stores.)

Mix tempera paint in small amounts, about the consistency of thick cream. Or you may use printing ink. Pour small amounts onto paper plates. Use a separate paper plate for each color. Do not make the paint too deep, or the design will lose some of its intricacy.

Wet the sponges in water and wring them out. They should be just damp.

Show each child how to place each sponge into the tempera paint, then press onto the paper to make a print. Encourage the children to combine the shapes and colors in whatever fashion they desire.

You might want to have the children make Easter cards for the congregation.

Bethlehem

Craft 1

Supplies: animalitoes (see page 78), scissors, crayons or markers, small circles cut from construction paper, glue, yarn, stapler and staples, cotton balls or facial tissue (optional: cotton fabric, needle and thread)

Make Animalitoes

Make two copies of the animalitoes (see page 78) for each child in your group.

Say: Christmas is a holiday that people all over the world celebrate. Each country celebrates in a different way. Today we are going to make a special decoration. The expert weavers of Guatemala make these animalitoes (animal EE toes), or *little animals*, from hand-woven cotton fabric. The animalitoes are shaped like dogs, donkeys, sheep, elephants, bulls, and rabbits. But today, since we are going to be talking about the trip to Bethlehem, our animalitoes will look like sheep or donkeys. (If you have a globe, show the children where Guatemala is.)

Ask: What does a donkey have to do with a trip to Bethlehem? (*Invite the children to share the donkey's role.*) How does the sheep relate to the Christmas story? (*Shepherds heard the news of Jesus' birth first.*)

Have the children cut out the two sides of the animal each chooses to make. Place the two sides so that their noses face each other. Then let the children decorate the outside of their animals with stripes, squiggles, or other designs. Have them make both animal pieces the same. Add dark, round eyes to both pieces.

Once the outside is decorated, let the children create a tail and mane from the yarn scraps. Glue to the inside of one of the halves. With the crayon side out, staple the two pieces together around the bottom half.

At the opening, stuff the animal with cotton balls or facial tissue. When sufficiently stuffed, staple closed. Tie a length of yarn around the donkey's neck. Form a loop to hang on the Christmas tree.

Bible
Luke
2:1-5

If you have a longer time, the children may make their animalitoes out of cotton fabric. Instead of stapling around the edges, let the children stitch around the edges with a needle and thread.

craft z

Supplies: aluminum pie plates, newspapers, nails, hammer, pre-gathered Christmas trim, colored yarn, white paper, pencil, permanent markers, tape, scissors, glue

Punched Tin Ornaments

Punched tin is a special craft often found in Mexico or Central America. Let the children make special ornaments to display in your classroom or to take home with them.

Trace around the bottom of each pie tin on a piece of white paper. Cut the circle out of the paper. This will become the template for the punched tin design.

Let the children create a design using pencil dots. They may make it as simple or as elaborate as they want.

Poke through each dot in the designs with a sharp pencil. Tape the design to the inside of the pie plate. Then let the children use permanent markers to transfer the hole pattern to their pie plates.

Place the pie pan on a stack of newspaper on the floor. Have an adult hold the pan while the child uses a hammer and nail to punch through each dot.

Punch two holes, side by side, at the top of the plate. Thread a length of yarn through the holes and tie to form a hanger.

Let the children glue pre-gathered Christmas trim under the edge of the pie plate. Hang the ornaments as a greeting for all Christmas visitors.

Shepherds Visit Jesus

Craft 1

Supplies: muslin, newspaper, yellow and white crayons, water, three dishpans, food coloring, spoon, old towels, iron and ironing board; old silk ties, old clean pantyhose, or braided yarn

Let's Be Shepherds

Cut a one-yard square of plain muslin for each child. Cover the tables with newspaper. Set out yellow and white crayons. If you have a large class, make head ties. (Each child would need a six-by- thirty-six-inch strip of fabric.) Place water in each of the three dishpans. Add food coloring until the water is an intense color. Set the dishpans on tables covered with newspaper.

Give each child the square (or strip) of muslin.

> **Say:** Today we are going to be shepherds. Shepherds played an important role in the story of Jesus' birth. In order to be good shepherds, we have to look like shepherds. In order to look like shepherds, we need headdresses. We are going to decorate our headdresses using a technique called batik.

Let the children create a simple design with the yellow or white crayons. Dip the fabric in one of the dishpans of water and food coloring. Use a spoon to swish the fabric around. Continue swishing until the fabric is the color you want. Remove the fabric from the color bath and dip into the clear water. Wring out and then place the fabric between sheets of newspaper or old towels and blot. If you have time, repeat this process with another color of dye. Iron the fabric dry. Change the newspaper frequently to absorb the wax. The design will show through the colors.

When the time comes to wear the head- dresses, make a tie to secure them in place. Old silk ties, braided yarn, and clean discard- ed pantyhose make good ties. Tie around each child's head, securing the headdress in place.

Bible
Luke
2:8–20

© 1998 Abingdon Press.

craft 2

Supplies: black construction paper, crayons or markers, glitter, glue, glue brush, shallow tray or box lid

Good News Cards

Say: One of the ways we share the good news of Jesus' birth is to make special cards to send to people during this time of year. Let's make cards that will tell the story of the angels and the shepherds.

Give each child a piece of black construction paper. Have each child fold his or her paper in half to make a card. Let the children draw a picture of the shepherds on the front of the card. Place over a shallow tray or box lid. Then let children add glue to the sky and sprinkle glitter over it.

Say: We don't know what the angels looked like. We don't know if they were boys or girls or whether they had wings or were white and shining. But certainly they were a great sight because they convinced the shepherds that indeed God's only son had been born.

craft 3

Supplies: black construction paper, scissors, glue, white paper bags, cotton balls, special treats, handmade gift items

Make Goody Bags

Say: Let's make a special treat for friends and neighbors. Let's make goody bags that look like sheep.

Cut ears from black construction paper. Have the children glue the ears onto either side of a white paper bag. Cut out and glue on a nose and eyes. Glue on cotton balls to make the sheep wooly.

Let the children fill their bags with special handmade notepads, tasty treats, soaps, a hand-drawn picture, and a Bible verse card.

Say: Share your bag with a special friend.

Fishermen in Bible Times

craft 1

Supplies: colored tissue, plastic wrap, liquid starch in a cup, scissors, tape, paintbrush, newspaper

Fish Windows

Cut a piece of plastic wrap to fit your classroom window. Tape the corners of the wrap to newspaper.

Cut bits of colored art tissue into fish shapes and other ocean shapes (seaweed, coral, shells, and so forth). Spread these out on a table. Let the children place the shapes on the plastic wrap until they have created a fish window scene. Remove the shapes.

Paint starch over the plastic wrap. Let the children place the colored tissue pieces back on the plastic wrap and into the starch. Paint over the tissue pieces with more starch. Keep adding tissue designs until your fish window is complete.

Let the project dry completely. (This usually takes an hour or so.) Remove the tape or cut it at the corners of the plastic. Tape the plastic wrap fish window to a window in your classroom and watch the light shine through.

Bible
Luke
5:1–11

craft 2

Supplies: fine beach sand, cornstarch, water, double boiler, flat pan or cookie sheet

Sand—Clay Fish

Let the children help you mix 1 cup fine beach sand with ½ cup cornstarch. Pour the mixture into the top of a double boiler on the stove. Add ½ cup or a little more of boiling water and mix well.

Cook the sand-clay mixture in the double boiler briefly until thickened. (If it is too thick, add a little more boiling water.) Cool the clay a bit before modeling.

Let the children create sand-clay fish. Then place the sand clay fish on a flat pan in a 275-degree oven until dry. Or you can dry the sand-clay fish for several days on a shelf or table.

craft 3

Supplies: blender, measuring cup, water, torn newspaper, torn tissue paper, strainer, large shells, non-stick baking spray, sponges, paper towels

Fish Paper Molds

Mix together in a blender about 4 cups of water and ¼ cup of torn newspaper. Add some torn tissue paper for color. Put the lid on and blend. Then strain the watery paper pulp, removing as much water as possible.

Spray large shells with non-stick baking spray. Let the children press the paper pulp into the shells. Have them press firmly to make sure that each of the indentations is filled.

Have the children blot the pulp with a sponge to remove excess water. Place a paper towel on top of the mold. Place the shell mold in a warm place and dry thoroughly. Remove the dried colorful paper pulp forms from the shells.

Homes in Bible Times

craft 1

Supplies: shoeboxes, Bible storybooks, tape or glue, lightweight cardboard, scissors, modeling clay, chenille stems, fabric scraps

Bible—Times House

Let the children make Bible-times houses from shoeboxes. Do a little research before you begin. Most Bible storybooks contain pictures of houses from Bible times. Have those on hand for the children to look at, if they choose.

Give each child a shoebox, with the lid removed. Have the children turn their boxes upside-down. The bottom of the box will now be the roof of the house. Have them tape or glue the lid of the shoebox upside-down on the roof to form a railing. (This railing would have prevented people from accidentally falling off the roof.)

Let the children make an outside staircase by folding a strip of lightweight cardboard accordion-style. Have them tape the strip in place. Cut out one or two small windows and a door. (This may need to be done by an adult.)

Have the children make a small room or a booth on the flat roof. They can add sleeping mats and tiny water jugs made from modeling clay. They can make people from chenille stems and scraps of fabric. (Refer to your Bible storybooks for examples of how people dressed in Bible times.)

Bible
Luke
6:48-49

83

Craft 2

Supplies: welcome mat (see page 85), colored art tissue, glue, tagboard

Welcome Mat

Make a copy of the welcome mat (see page 85) for each child in the group. This will provide the template for the welcome mat the children will create. Glue the template to a piece of tagboard and trim around the edges.

Say: It is important to make people feel welcome. A visitor in Bible times was considered a gift from God. Today we often put a "Welcome" mat outside our doors to tell people that visitors will be made welcome. It is nice to know when you are a stranger that there will be a place where you can feel welcome.

Have the children decide what colors they will want to use for their welcome mats. Provide colored art tissue. (Scraps will work well for this activity.) Cut or tear the tissue paper into small squares about two inches across. Tear out many shapes prior to starting, so that you don't have to stop frequently to do this. This will keep the activity moving quickly.

Let children decide which area of the welcome mat they will begin to work with. Wad up a square of tissue paper, dip it lightly in the glue, and then place it on the template.

Hint: Make the letters of the word *Welcome* first, before beginning the rest of the design.

Place the little wads of tissue paper very close together so that they will form a "mat" appearance.

Set aside the welcome mats to dry when the children have finished them. Place them in the hallway around the door of the classroom, or let the children take them home to place where visitors can easily see them once they are dry.

© 2000 Abingdon Press.

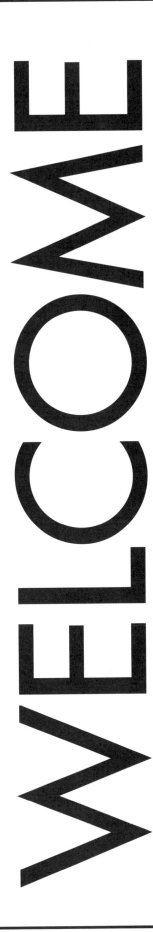

Shepherds in Bible Times

craft

Supplies: eighteen-inch squares of sturdy cardboard, utility knife, rubber bands

Make a Shepherd's Harp

Before class begins, cut a "C" shape from cardboard. Make the letter approximately three inches thick. This will provide the harp base. Cut four or five "V" notches in the top curve of the "C" and matching ones in the bottom curve.

Say: Shepherds often played musical instruments as a way of passing the long hours away from their villages. Certainly the sound of flute or harp music provided a calming effect on the easily excitable sheep. Let's make our own shepherd's harps.

Give each child his or her harp base. Show the children how to string rubber bands between the top and bottom notches.

Let the children strum their shepherd's harps.

© 1997 Abingdon Press.

Bible
Luke
15:4-7

86

Jesus' Baptism

craft 1

Supplies: pencil, paper, plastic sandwich bags, three-dimensional fabric paint

Make a Dove Magnet

Trace a simple outline of a dove, using the outline below. Photocopy one for each child.

Slip the drawings inside plastic sandwich bags. Using white three-dimensional fabric paint, let the children outline the dove. Then have them fill in the dove, making sure all the spaces are filled.

Bible
John
1:29-34

Set the doves aside and let them dry for three or four days.

Let the children peel the doves from the bags. They will adhere to plastic and metal without requiring a magnet.

craft z

Supplies: dove glider (see page 89), watercolor markers, dishpan or cotton swabs, water, masking tape (optional: paper towels, iron and ironing board)

Art Effects

Make a copy of the dove glider (see page 89) for each child in the group. This glider will be used in a game, so do the decorating early to give the gliders time to dry. If you find the gliders are not dry by the time you are ready to fold them and fly them, place each piece of paper between paper towels and iron until it is dry. This will require adult supervision.

Have the children color their dove gliders using watercolor markers. Encourage each to cover the entire design. Then provide them an option as to how to use the water. They may dip their entire papers into the dishpan of water and allow the colors to run together. They may take cotton swabs and dip them into water, and then rub them over their designs. A third choice might be to hold the paper with two hands, have a friend drip water onto it, and then tilt it back and forth to let the water run in pleasing ways.

> **Say:** Not only do we hear a story from the Bible that talks about water being something very special, but we also learn how the dove became the symbol of our church for the Holy Spirit. All those who were present at Jesus' baptism knew that Jesus was God's son.

When the dove gliders are dry, show the children how to fold the gliders (like a paper airplane).

> **Say:** The dove has become the symbol of the Holy Spirit because of what happened to Jesus when he was baptized by John. (*Recall how the Holy Spirit came down on Jesus like a dove when he came up from the water after being baptized.*) Let's play a game. Let's see if you can get your dove gliders to land in the circle that I will create on the floor.

Use masking tape to create a space on the floor. Make it large enough for the doves to fit inside. Pace off a distance of about six to ten feet. Mark a starting line at that point. The children can throw the doves as often as they like, but they must stay behind the line while throwing. Whenever a child's dove lands inside the circle, the child will say: "Jesus is the Son of God."

If you have a large group, you may want to create several circles and divide the children into groups of six participants. That way each child will have time to throw several times.

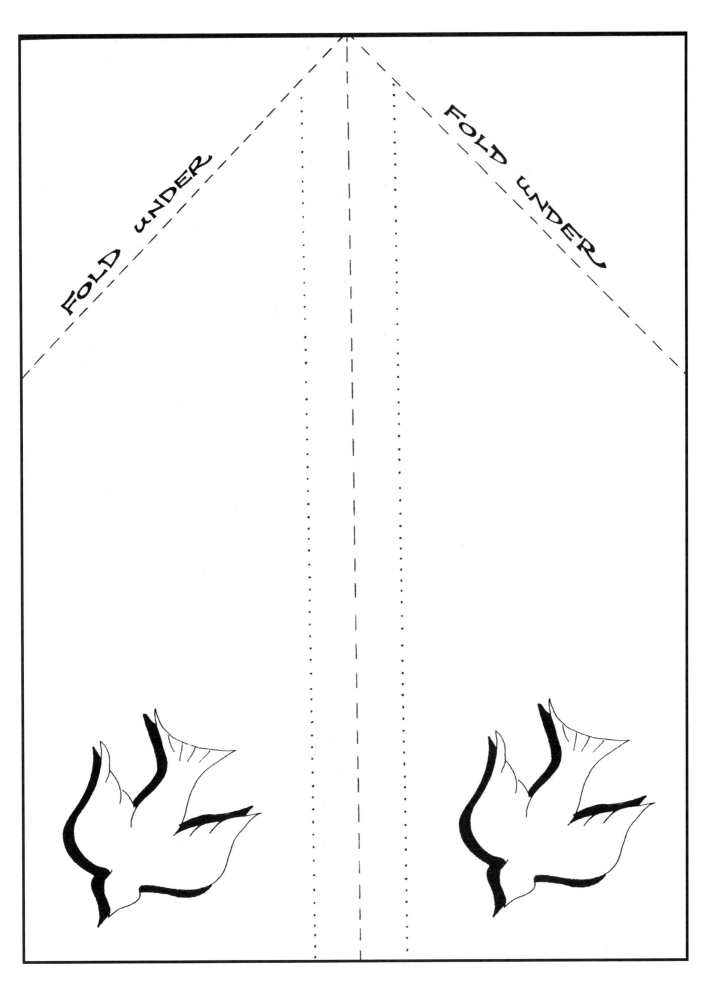

FOLD UNDER

FOLD UNDER

The Man Beside the Pool

craft 1

Supplies: powdered tempera paint, clear dishwashing liquid, water, separate bowls or jars, newspaper, drinking straws, white paper

Bubble Trouble

Before class begins, create the bubble paint for the activity. To make bubble paint mix ¼ cup powdered tempera paint, 2 teaspoons clear dishwashing liquid, and 3 tablespoons water. To intensify the colors, add more tempera paint.

Put each color in a separate bowl or jar. Make sure each child has access to one bowl of paint. Cover the work surfaces with newspaper.

Ask: Have you ever wanted to capture a bubble? Did you ever try? Did you succeed? We can't keep a bubble from bursting, but we can capture its print on paper. Today we're talking about a place where bubbles were very important. They changed a plain pool of water into a pool that healed illnesses. Let's play with bubbles today and capture a few on paper.

Give each child a drinking straw and a piece of white paper (six-inch square). Remind the children not to share straws but to wipe off straws if anyone decides to change colors.

Say: Gently blow the straw into the bubble paint mixture. Absolutely do not suck in. The mixture tastes terrible and might make you sick. Keep blowing until the bubbles overflow. To capture a bubble print gently roll your piece of paper on top of the bubbles. When you have finished capturing all the bubbles you want, lay the paper flat to dry. You might want to try using two or more colors.

Bible
John
5:2-9

craft 2

Supplies: white tissue paper, liquid starch, pencils, empty egg carton, felt-tip markers

Make a Prayer Pencil Topper

Let the children make prayer pencil toppers.

To make tissue paper mash, use several sheets of white tissue paper and liquid starch. Let the children tear the tissue paper into small pieces. Add enough starch to wet the paper.

Press the concoction into a firm glob. Squeeze out the excess starch.

Let the children take turns squeezing the glob until it feels like a workable dough.

Have each child mold a small glob of tissue paper mash into a simple head shape. The mash will be lumpy, so it will be a little tricky to work with. Have each child insert a pencil into the neck of the head shape.

Encourage the children to continue to mold their creations until they look the way the children want them to.

Stick the pencil, with the topper still attached, into the backside of an empty egg carton to dry.

When the toppers are dry, let the children decorate them with felt-tip markers.

   Say: Use your pencil topper to remind yourself to pray for your friends.

The Boy's Lunch

craft

Supplies: lunch pouch and loaves and fishes cards (see page 93), paper punch, yarn, scissors, masking tape, crayons or felt-tip markers,

A Lunch for Sharing

Make a copy of the lunch pouch (see page 93) for each child. The scrip represents a leather pouch that might have been what the boy in the Bible story carried his lunch in.

Say: Today we're talking about a special lunch and how it multiplied to feed more than five thousand people. We might wonder how that happened. But with God anything is possible. God took a small boy's gift and multiplied it many times. God can do that with what we have to share too.

Show the children how to fold the scrip and punch holes along the edges. Cut the yarn into one-yard lengths, one for each child. Wrap the end with a piece of masking tape to make it easy to use. Leaving a twelve-inch tail, lace the scrip together. Tie the end pieces together, forming a handle that will fit easily over a child's head, and let the scrip hang down.

Have the children cut apart the loaves and fishes cards and place them in the pouch. If you have an extended time, let the children decorate the pouch with crayons or felt-tip markers.

Bible
John
6:1-14

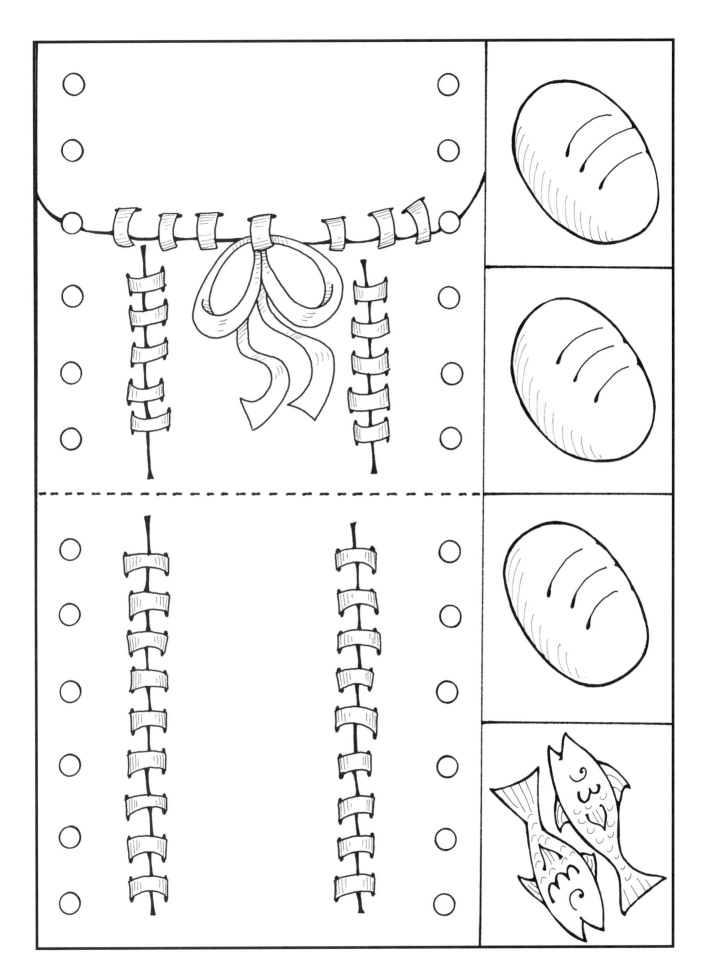

93

Palm Sunday

craft 1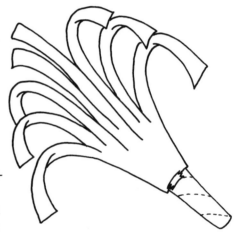

Supplies: green construction paper, cardboard tubes, tape, scissors

Shake It Up!

Say: When Jesus rode into Jerusalem, the people broke off palm branches and waved them as he passed by. Since we don't have any palm branches, we will create our own to honor Jesus as he rides into Jerusalem for the Passover. These shakers will be our palm branches.

Give each child a piece of green construction paper and a cardboard tube. (Use cardboard tubes that come inside paper towels, wrapping paper, or bathroom tissue. After the activity, remove the construction paper and store the tubes for another use in other lessons.)

Have the children tape the construction paper around the wide end of the tube as shown here. Cut in from the outside edge of the construction paper to the edge of the cardboard tube.

© 1998 Abingdon Press.

Have the children use these shakers as palm branches to tell the story of Jesus' triumphal entry into Jerusalem.

© 1998 Abingdon Press.

Bible
John
12:12-15

94

craft z

Supplies: palm branch (see page 96), crayons or markers, scissors, glue or tape, drinking straws or wooden dowels

Playful Palms

Invite the children to the tables. Give each child a copy of the palm branch (see page 96).

Say: In the place where Jesus grew up, date palms grew in great abundance. There was even a city known as the City of Palms, because there was a seven-mile-long grove of palms that lined the main road to it.

Ask: What do you think of when you see a palm tree? (*beaches, tropical places, vacations*)

Say: The palm was a welcome sign to weary travelers in Bible times, as well. It usually signaled an oasis where travelers and camels could sit in the shade and perhaps get a cool drink of water. The palm leaves were also used to honor important people as they traveled along the road. People would break off the leaves and wave them in the air. Today we are going to make palm branches.

Have the children color and cut out their palm leaves. Cut along the lines indicated. Then show the children how to glue (or tape) the drinking straws or wooden dowels down the center parts of the leaves, making handles of the ends extending beyond the leaves.

When the palm leaves are complete, have the children practice waving them.

Say: Let's wave the leaves high and joyfully. (*Pause and give the children time to do this.*) Let's wave them low and slowly. (*Pause and give the children time to do this.*) Let's wave them all about and shout "Hosanna!" (*Pause and give the children time to do this.*)

Say: The palm branch has become the symbol of a special day in our church. It is called Palm Sunday. On this day Jesus rode into Jerusalem on a donkey and the people greeted him with palm branches.

Permission granted to photocopy for local church use. © 1999 Abingdon Press.

Peter's Denial

Craft

Supplies: rooster suncatcher picture (see page 98), dinner-size paper plates, scissors, glue or tape, paper punch, yarn, newspaper, baby oil or vegetable oil, small dish, cotton swabs, crayons or felt-tip markers, paper towels (optional: iron and ironing board)

Let the Sunshine In

Prior to class make a copy of the rooster suncatcher picture (see page 98) for each child. Cut out the centers of dinner-size paper plates. Make sure the area will accommodate the rooster picture, with space left over to glue or tape the edges down. Punch two holes at the top of each plate. Thread a six-inch length of yarn through the holes and tie the ends to create a hanger.

Cover the tables with newspaper. On each table place these items: a small dish of baby oil (or vegetable oil), cotton swabs, crayons or felt-tip markers, rooster pictures, paper plates, and tape or glue.

Say: Today we're talking about a very special animal. This animal makes a special sound, and its sound reminded one of Jesus's friends that he had not stood up for his friend Jesus. We are going to make a suncatcher that we can hang up and remind us to stand up for Jesus.

Let the children color the picture with crayons or felt-tip markers. When all the areas have been colored, let the children lay the picture face down on the newspaper. Dip a cotton swab in oil and lightly rub back and forth over the reverse side of the picture. Blot with paper towels. Allow to dry. (Ironing the picture while it is covered with a paper towel will hasten the drying process.) While the picture dries, let the children decorate the edges of the paper plate. Tape the rooster picture behind the center of the plate. Trim to fit into the circle.

Ask: What does a rooster sound like? (*Let the children crow.*) Can you crow any louder? (*Encourage the children to really crow loudly.*) This sound was so powerful that it reminded Peter that he had broken a promise to Jesus.

Bible
John
18:15-18, 25-27

97

Pentecost

craft 1

Supplies: fish trumpet (see page 101), scissors, crayons or markers, cardboard tubes, white glue, tape, colored tissue paper, rubber bands, sharp pencils or toothpicks

Fish Trumpets

Make a copy of the fish trumpet pattern (see page 101) for each pair of children in the group.

Have the children cut apart the two trumpet covers. At this point they can decorate the fish background in any way they choose. Or they may use crayons or markers. Cover a cardboard tube in white glue. Fit the fish trumpet cover around the outside of the cardboard tube. Trim as necessary. To avoid mess you may want to tape the cover around the tube. Tape one end to the cardboard tube, roll the design around the tube, and then tape the opposite end.

Cut colored tissue paper into four-inch circles. Place one circle over the end of the cardboard tube and secure it with a rubber band. With a sharp pencil or a toothpick, poke several holes in the tissue paper.

   Say: Today when we sing our song of celebration, we are going to make a joyful noise with our fish trumpets.

Let the children practice humming into their trumpets. The tissue paper will vibrate and make a humming sound. Have the children march around the room humming into their trumpets.

   Say: This is the way that Peter must have felt when he was filled with the Holy Spirit. It was humming inside and wanting to get out. So Peter let it out as he told the people about Jesus.

© 2000 Abingdon Press.

Bible
Acts
2:1-4

craft 2

Supplies: one-pint cardboard ice cream cartons, acrylic spray paint (red), red ribbon, scissors, permanent felt-tip markers, paper punch, and yarn

Pentecost Wind Catcher

Say: The color for Pentecost is red. Often we use mobiles and hanging spirals to remind us that the Holy Spirit came with wind and flame. Let's make a Pentecost wind catcher to remind you that God sent the Holy Spirit to be a teacher, helper, comforter, and empowerer.

Before class begins, remove the bottoms of the cartons. Wash and dry the ice cream cartons. Spray them both inside and out with the red paint. This may take several coats to create an even surface.

Give each child a carton. Let each child use a paper punch to punch two holes opposite each other on the bottom edges. Give each child a piece of yarn about twelve inches long. Have the children tie one end through each hole. This will be the top of the wind catcher.

Let your children draw symbols on the carton with permanent felt-tip markers. Punch holes along the bottom edges. Space them evenly. Cut red ribbon about twenty-four inches long. Help the children attach a piece of ribbon at each hole.

Say: Hang up the wind catcher to remind yourself that the Holy Spirit can guide you and encourage you to share the story of Jesus with others.

101

We Are Called Christians

craft

Supplies: finger fish pattern (see page 103), crayons or markers, scissors, glue or stapler and staples

Finger Fish

Give each child a copy of the finger fish pattern (see page 103). Each pattern will make one finger fish.

Have the children color and cut out the fish. Attach the side fins. Assemble the finger fish by stapling or gluing both sides of the fish together.

Leave a small opening at the bottom where the children will insert two fingers so that the fish finger puppet will sit on their hands.

   Say: The fish has become a symbol of persons who believe in Jesus. This is partly true because the first persons Jesus called were the fishermen.

© 2000 Abingdon Press.

Bible
Acts
11:26

Attach fin

Attach fin

Lydia

craft

Supplies: construction paper, scissors, felt-tip markers or crayons

Spread the Word

Let the children in your class make good news door hangers.

Give each child a sheet of construction paper about five inches wide by ten inches long. Help each child cut a hole in his or her construction paper large enough to go over a doorknob.

Have each child write a special message on his or her hanger, such as: "God loves you" or "Jesus is my friend."

Say: You can place the door hangers on a doorknob in your house to remind yourself to tell the good news.

Bible
Acts
16:13-15

Paul and Silas in Prison

craft

Supplies: kingdom keys (see page 106), crayons or markers, scissors, stapler and staples, tape

Kingdom Keys

Say: Paul and Silas didn't need keys to get them out of prison. God was with them, and God kept them safe.

Ask: How did Paul and Silas use their time in prison to spread the message of Jesus? (*They sang hymns and prayed.*) Why did the jailer plan to kill himself? (*He was afraid all the prisoners had escaped.*) Had they? (*No; they were still in their cells.*) What did the jailer do? (*He took Paul and Silas home with him and tended their wounds.*) What happened when Paul and Silas told the jailer about Jesus? (*He believed and became a follower of Jesus.*)

Say: God sent Jesus into the world so that people could understand how they were supposed to live and how they were supposed to treat one another. Jesus died to save us and to give us the keys to God's kingdom. Let's make keys to the kingdom that we can share with other people.

Give each child a copy of the kingdom keys (see page 106). Show the children how to color the keys, cut them out, and fold them. Staple or tape the two sides together. Then cut out the Bible verses.

Choose one or more Bible verses to go in each kingdom key pocket. Let the children hand out the pockets in church or to their friends or to other persons they meet.

Bible
Acts
16:22–30

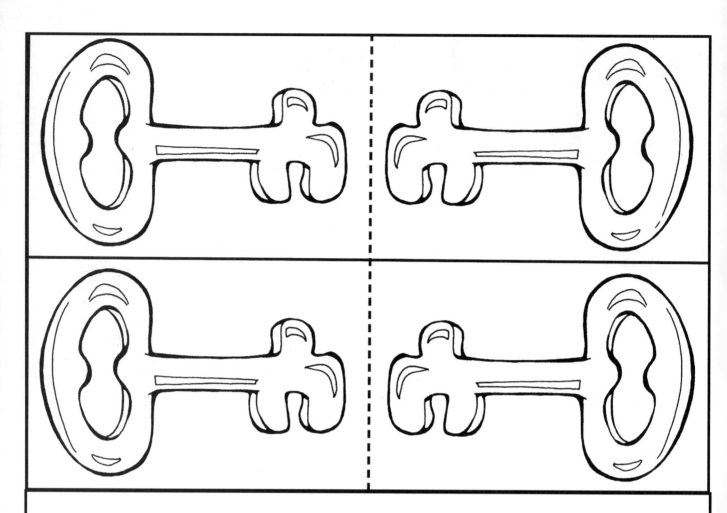

Believe in the Lord Jesus, and you will be saved.
Acts 16:31, Good News Bible

For God so loved the world that he gave his only Son,
so that everyone who believes in him may not perish
but may have eternal life. John 3:16

Blessed are those who have not seen
and yet have come to believe.
John 20:29

Jesus said to them,"But who do you say that I am?"
Simon Peter answered, "You are the Messiah,
the Son of the living God." Matthew 16:15-16, adapted

Love One Another

craft

Supplies: construction paper in several different colors, pencil, scissors, paper punch, white glue, sandpaper, clear nail polish, cotton swabs, twelve- to twenty-four inches of silk or leather cord per child

Make a Paper Pendant

Before class begins draw a heart about two inches wide on a piece of construction paper and cut it out. Trace the cutout over and over on several pieces of different-colored construction paper.

Let the children cut out each heart until each has a stack of the exact same heart, about one inch thick. Let each child use a paper punch to make a hole in the exact same place on each paper heart, somewhere near the heart's center. (They can stack a few pieces at a time and punch them all at once.)

Have the children glue the heart shapes on top of each other, making sure the holes line up.

Set the hearts aside to dry overnight.

Show the children how to sand around the edges of their stack of hearts at an angle.

> **Say:** You can sand some places more than others so new colors will show. The more sanded your heart is, the better it will look.

When the children have sanded their hearts as much as they like, have them thread a length of silk or leather cord through their hearts. (Paint the ends of the cord with clear nail polish to keep them from coming unraveled.) Help them tie the cord in a knot.

> **Say:** Give one to a friend who doesn't know about Jesus. Then tell the person the good news.

Bible
Romans
13:8

Paul's Letters

Craft 1

Supplies: posterboard; scissors; feathers, lace, sequins, beads, buttons, or other craft materials; magnetic tape strip; glue

Stuck on Love

Cut heart shapes from posterboard. Make one for each child in the class. Let the children make stick-up magnets to put on metal surfaces to remind them to love one another. Have the children decorate the hearts with feathers, lace, sequins, beads, buttons, or any other craft materials you have available.

Cut one-inch strips from a roll of magnetic tape. Glue the tape to the backs of the hearts. Let the children take them home to put on their refrigerators or metal surfaces in their houses. If they have lockers at school, they can place the magnets there as a reminder to love one another.

© 1999 Abingdon Press.

Craft 2

Supplies: love notes plane (see page 109), crayons or markers

Launching Love Notes

Photocopy the love notes plane (see page 109) for each child in the class.

Say: There are many people who need to know that God loves them. We can take these paper airplanes with us and send them to people who might not know God's love.

Let the children color their airplanes. Fold the planes. Have contests to see which child's plane goes the farthest, which stays in the air the longest, and so forth. If you plan a mass flight from the balcony of the sanctuary, let the children make extra planes.

Bible
Romans 13:8;
Philippians
1:1-2

© 1999 Abingdon Press.

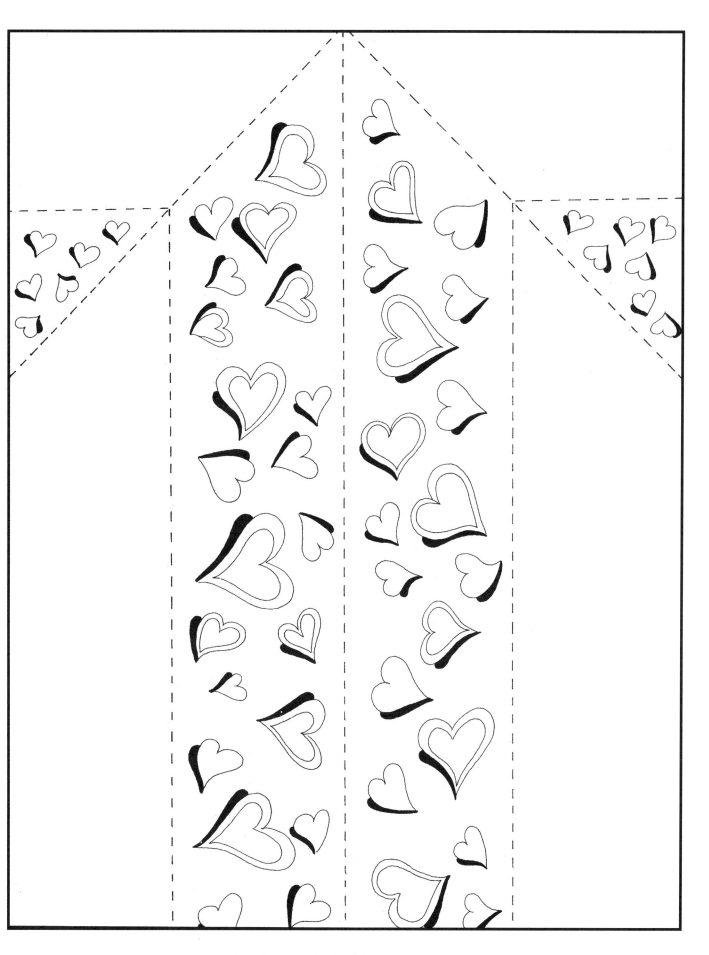

Timothy

craft

Supplies: dark-colored posterboard, scissors, aluminum foil, pens or pencils, glue (optional: flashlight, mirror)

Reflections of Glory

Say: Timothy was a young boy who helped Paul tell others the story of Jesus. Timothy might have been young, but he was able to set an example for other people to follow. He was kind, he was loving, he was helpful, and he was faithful. He was a reflection of all that Jesus had taught.

Cut a piece of posterboard into four 8½-by-11-inch cards. Give each child a card and a piece of aluminum foil. Let the children trace or draw interesting shapes onto the foil. Then cut out the shapes, keeping the foil as smooth as possible. Glue the aluminum shapes shiny side up and close together on the card.

If it is a sunny day, take the cards outside or place them under a bright light to see the light reflect off the foil and onto other surfaces. Encourage the children to take these home and go outside at night. Shine a flashlight on the foil cards, reflecting the designs onto a wall or door. You can also try reflecting the shapes into a mirror.

Say: As Christians we are called to be reflections of Jesus' teachings. When we treat others with kindness, when we share, when we are loving, when we are faithful, just like Timothy did, we have set an example for others to follow. Then we are each reflections of Jesus' life.

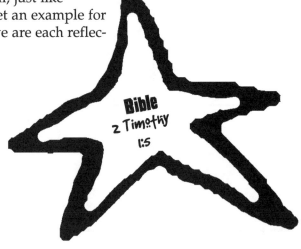

Bible
2 Timothy
1:5

Index by Bible Reference

Index by Subject